From Paul *to* Philippi, *with* Love

From Paul *to* Philippi, *with* Love

by

Anna M. Griffith

So often we read a scripture
many, many times, and
through the years, we glean
many rubies from it.

Then one day we discover a diamond.

—Ron Bryant

ISBN: 0-89137-434-5

Dedication

This book is lovingly dedicated
to Bible students everywhere
whose hearts would reach out
to touch those of the
Philippian Christians.

Acknowledgments

Many, many thanks to...

...Ron Bryant, George Covalt, and Jean Moffatt, for their careful, loving, and critical readings of this manuscript.

...Carl Griffith, for loving support, understanding, long-suffering, and encouragement.

Table of Contents

Introduction

I have often thought that some of the best Bible students we have in the church are our women, especially those who are active in ladies' Bible classes. Anna Griffith is such a student. She has been active in teaching Bible classes most of her adult Christian life. She is well-acquainted with books and study guides that are available and also recognizes areas wherein we are deficient in such materials. This book is her endeavor to fill one of those needs in ladies' Bible classes and other adult classes.

Paul's letter to the Philippian church has long been a favorite of New Testament students. Its beauty and practicality are easily recognized. Study guides for this epistle, however, have often taken the devotional track rather than the exegetical. Anna has sought to combine both approaches in these fourteen lessons. There is inspiration and beauty to be contemplated by the student who favors a more devotional approach to the book. And on the other side, there is a serious study of the key Greek words in the epistle, giving the more exacting student ample material for discussion and for thought.

Each chapter is followed by thought-provoking questions which will supply much food for a discussion-type class, and the private student will be benefited by "thinking on these things."

This is a new and different approach to an old and much-loved letter.

Harvey Porter
Albuquerque, New Mexico

Preface

The book of Philippians in the New Testament is a "charmer," if you will. With the possible exception of one outstanding passage (Philippians 2:5-11), it contains no vast theological treatise, no stern rebuke, and no impassioned plea of repentance from grave sin. It was a letter born of gratitude and deep affection—and one often overlooked by Bible school curriculum committees.

This volume does not purport to bring out any new truths about the letter. The purpose is merely to point out areas which the author considers relevant to today's Christian reader and today's Christian churches.

The exhortation to teachers is stern: "Let not many of you become teachers, my brethren, knowing that as such we shall incur a stricter judgment. For we all stumble in many ways." (James 3:1,2a). Every teacher, preacher, and elder teaches from the ideal—what the situation should be, what a life should manifest, and the goal for which we *should* strive. This author is no different; the goals set forth are hers, the challenges personal, and the ideals subjective.

The needs of the church today are the same as they were in the first century—to be one, to reach Heaven with the help of one another, and to grow into the Lord's image on earth. Paul's letter to the Philippians addressed that need for them, and it addresses this need for us. A reconsideration is most certainly in order.

—Anna M. Griffith

Textual Note: Except as noted, biblical quotations appearing in this manuscript have been taken from the New American Standard Version.

I

The Molder

God Will Bring Us Around If We Let Him

Text. . . . . Philippians 1:1-11.

Supplementary.....Philippians 2:12,13, 3:9,15, 4:13.

Memory Verse. . . . . Philippians 1:6.

For years after becoming a Christian, I was taught that I should grow into Christ's image, to become like Him, to love as He loved, to exhibit His patience and forbearance, etc. In order to do this, I was to study to show myself approved (2 Timothy 2:15). I was to add to my faith (which came from hearing, which came from the Word of God) virtue, to virtue knowledge, to knowledge self-control, to self-control steadfastness, to steadfastness godliness, to godliness brotherly affection, and to brotherly affection love (2 Peter 1:5-7). All of this is scripture, of course, and to the best of my ability, I should follow these injunctions with diligence and sincerity. But something was lacking. I studied, still feeling myself to be a workman unapproved. I was a victim of the "do this, and do this, but don't do that" syndrome. I tried to climb the ladder of these marvelous Christian graces, one rung at a time, only to find that when I got to the middle of the ladder—usually about "steadfastness"—my faith and virtue were so wobbly, I would have to go back to them to shore them up, never seeming to make it to the top rung of "love." Discouragement settled firmly in place, eventually being replaced by apathy. Christian growth had become a pipe dream, and the joy that Paul spoke of repeatedly in Philippians seemed to be just something that was given to the primitive Christians by direct revelation. I couldn't do it myself.

Meanwhile, the "Please, God; I can do it myself" mindset still prevailed in my everyday walk of life. I felt that I knew how to rear my children, handle people, and conduct myself in any situation. One by one, these myths fell before my crumbling altar of self-sufficiency, and I began to acknowledge, "Help, Lord; I cannot do it myself." And day by day, as I committed more and more of my activities into heavenly hands, God responded, "Dear stubborn child; you know my way is best. Take my yoke upon you and learn from me; for I am gentle and lowly in heart, and you will find rest for your soul. For my yoke is easy, and my burden is light."

THE SOLUTION

Paul in his writings time and time again tells us that God is the one who empowers us with the ability to grow. He gives us the strength and the direction. In no other book is this more evident than in Paul's epistle to the Philippians.

HE FINISHES WHAT HE STARTS

> *For I am confident of this very thing that He who began a good work in you will perfect it until the day of Christ Jesus.*
>
> *—Philippians 1:6*

God can be counted on to finish something once He starts it. Often the only thing keeping Him from working in the Christian is simply unbelief.

HE DEVELOPS THE FRUITS OF SALVATION IN OUR LIVES

> *So then, my beloved, just as you have always obeyed, not as in my presence only, but now much more in my absence, work out your salvation with fear and trembling; for it is God who is at work in you, both to will and to do for His good pleasure.*
>
> *—Philippians 2:12,13*

There are two interpretations usually given for Philippians 2:12. The first is that one is given the mandate here to do and to think as he chooses in regard to his own salvation; in other words, that he can design the terms of his salvation. This cannot be true, however, since God has designed the terms. And, anyway, those to whom Paul was writing were already saved.

The second is that if one works hard enough (i.e., performs enough righteous acts), he will be able to earn his salvation. If this be true, why did Jesus have to die? That sacrifice would have been unnecessary if individuals could be good enough to save themselves.

In the phrase "working out your own salvation," Paul uses the verb κατεργαδζομαι *(katergadzomai)*. It means "to effect, to produce, or to bring out as a result," and is used in Romans 4:15, Romans 5:13, Romans 7:13, 2 Corinthians 4:17, and others.

In 2 Corinthians 7:10, for example, we are told that godly sorrow *works itself out* in one's life to yield repentance to salvation.

So what Paul is really saying is this: "Let the mind of Christ so dwell in you that, with God's help working in you too, you will let this spirit lead you to right action in your life, leading to sanctification." The best way to interpret Philippians 2:12 is to say that because of our relationship with God, we can allow our salvation to make itself manifest in our lives.

Think of the most valuable possession you own in your house—perhaps the first thing you would try to save in a fire. Now imagine the most expensive thing you can visualize—the most expensive jewel in the world, the most elaborate structure, something that just costs so very much that you could never own it.

But *you* do own the most valuable thing in the world. It is so valuable that all the money in the world cannot purchase it. It is something that was bought, though, and the highest price that was ever paid for anything in history was paid for that priceless thing that you own. The God of Heaven paid the highest price ever given in any transaction—that of the life of His Son—to gain this valuable commodity for you, and then He gave it to you as a gift. It is your salvation! Grace—the free gift of God!

It is something that can never be taken from you, unless you will it to be. It affects everything you say, do, or think. It affects the way you dress, what you do with your time, how you rear your children, how you spend your money, and the way you treat other people.

Because you are in Christ, your salvation must be allowed to be worked out in your life. Make it evident; cultivate it; give it room to grow. Let it have its free course, "for it is God who is at work in you"—who energizes you and motivates you—"both to desire and accomplish *His* good pleasure."

HE MOLDS OUR ATTITUDES

> *Let us therefore, as many as are perfect, have this attitude; and if in anything you have a different attitude, God will reveal that also to you.*
>
> —*Philippians 3:15*

Which of us, in his meager struggles toward God's heart, can say precisely how God molds him? Just as we were unaware, from minute to minute, of our physical growth during childhood, so likely we are similarly unaware of true spiritual growth. Some have said that it is a continuing process of letting go, and letting God. Just as surely, it can be the timely application of a scripture heretofore unheeded.

Several times in my life, I have successfully taken as a project the task of reading the Bible straight through over a period of months. I *know* that I have read every scripture in the Bible. But the timeless beauty of this living Book consists in the fact that often, in studying a passage, my spiritual maturity of the moment will absorb a heretofore overlooked principle. Does the "I don't remember ever reading that scripture before" feeling seem familiar? It should. This could mean you are growing, and God is molding you. When you read it, recognizing its power or its message in a new light, are you then willing to put it into practice, letting it change your life? You should; this, then, could mean that you are willing to be molded.

HE TEACHES US TO LOVE

> *Now may our God and Father Himself and Jesus our Lord direct our way to you: And may the Lord cause you to increase and abound in love for one another, and for all men, just as we also do for you.*
>
> —*1 Thessalonians 3:11,12*

Now as to the love of the brethren, you have no need for anyone to write to you, for you yourselves are taught by God to love one another.

—1 Thessalonians 4:9

Does it matter if we understand *how* He teaches the Christian to love? Is it not simply marvelous that He can and does when we let Him?

Is there someone you don't like? There are people in my life that I have trouble liking. Not only that, there are people that I have trouble seeing—just ordinary people who blend in with the furniture, so to speak. "Oh, Father, forgive me! Help me to be aware of each and every one; help me to see the inside person as You see; help me to love with Your love; help me to behold the good and to be patient with the bad. Oh, Father, I want to love; help me with the part inside me that wants to cling to the un-love."

If we will admit to ourselves that we do not know fully what love is—and we do not...

And that God's love is perfect, rich, abundant, and full—which it is...

And that the only way we can show this love to the world is to let God's love shine in us—which it can...

Then let us pray sincerely and fervently that God will cleanse our hearts of all the little petty selfishness, envyings, jealousies, grievances, and irritations which keep us from letting God's love flow through our beings, and get on with the business of letting Him teach us to love!

HE ENABLES US TO LIVE POWERFULLY

Now to Him who is able to do exceeding abundantly beyond all that we ask or think, according to the power that works within us, to Him be the glory in the church and in Christ Jesus to all generations forever and ever.

—Ephesians 3:20,21

I can do all things through Him who strengthens me.

—Philippians 4:13

These are just more verses which teach us that God longs to work in our lives. They say that He is able to do so much more than we can ever imagine or are even able to ask for. These things can be done through His power working within us: not we ourselves acting alone, but God working far beyond our comprehension through us.

Where is our faith? Is it withered through lack of study? Has it atrophied through lack of use? God has promised to do His part.

HE HELPS US TO BE QUALIFIED

> *And such confidence we have through Christ toward God. Not that we are adequate in ourselves to consider anything as coming from ourselves, but our adequacy is from God, who also made us adequate as servants of a new covenant, not of the letter, but of the Spirit; for the letter kills, but the Spirit gives life.*
>
> *—2 Corinthians 3:4-6*

Do we feel inadequate to teach our neighbors? If we strive to make ourselves adequate, worrying about the eloquence of our speech, the effectiveness of our visual aids, and the humor that we insert—yes, we should feel inadequate. Do we feel inadequate to participate in a bus ministry, a counseling ministry, an inner-city mission work, a prison ministry, or whatever? We should, if our competence originates from our own endeavors or from the "Please, God; I'd rather do it myself" mindset.

But can we, like Paul, truthfully say that our adequacy is from God—that the grace, poise, and serenity we possess come from Him, because of our covenant relationship with Him? When we teach, do we teach Christ, or are we trying to put across how brilliant we are? Do we minister to show our selfish goodness? We are not competent to claim anything as coming from us, but our competence is from God. Fellow Christians, He has made *us* to be ministers of a New Covenant—not with creeds, or "how to" manuals, or church programs, but in the Spirit—in His Spirit, who does what He said the Spirit would do, in that the Spirit is with us, strengthening, comforting, and guiding, so that indeed we are competent to be His ministers.

Two other passages from the heart of 2 Corinthians—3:18 and 5:5—again emphasize that God is molding us, and this through His Spirit.

HE IS OUR SOURCE OF JOY, PEACE, AND HOPE

> *Now may the God of hope fill you with all joy and peace in believing, that you may abound in hope by the power of the Holy Spirit.*
>
> *—Romans 15:13*

Are we cutting off a very dynamic source for living because we do not avail ourselves of this joy and peace through the power of the Holy Spirit?

A person with whom I correspond wrote once, "All of us are the products of everything which has happened to us from the moment we were born until now." There is some truth to this. It sounds valid, but I wonder if this person really believes all that this statement implies. If this were entirely true, we would have no choices, but would simply be tossed by the elusive fates. Through our childhood years, of course, we were molded by what happened to us—intentionally and inadvertently. However, as we become adults, let us cast off that childish characteristic of being much affected by what happens to us, and determine that we shall choose that by which we continue to be molded.

Our bodies bear the choices of what we have chosen to consume—how much or how little, and what kind. When a person chooses to consume too much alcohol, he bears the consequences of alcoholism. When he chooses not to exercise, he bears the consequent flabbiness. When he chooses to read junk, or to absorb it through the media, he bears this fruit in his actions.

We are what we are through the decisions we make. To the extent that we decide that God shall be our supreme ruler, and to the extent that we can give up our wills to Him, this is the extent to which He will mold us. We need not be the products of everything which happens to us. With our wills surrendered to Him, WE HAVE THE OPTION TO BE THE PRODUCT OF EVERYTHING HE DECIDES THAT WILL AFFECT US.

When a traumatic event occurs, irreversibly altering the course of two lives, one life may be changed for the better, another for the worse. Why? Because one chooses to react in a different way than another. One allows the Holy Spirit to guide him so that his reaction is to some extent determined by the strength of the Spirit-filled Word within him. In line with this, we can consider one ramification of the very comforting scripture, Romans 8:28:

> *And we know that God causes all things to work together for good to those who love God, to those who are called according to His purpose.*

If we love God, we will let Him mold us. He can change a trauma in our lives into good because we allow Him to mold our reactions. If we can accept the trauma rather than deny it, going to God for His strength rather than becoming angry with Him and blaming it on Him, then our faith is counted as righteousness, and God can use this to strengthen us. One who chooses to "do it himself" cannot but react in a self-willed, perhaps vengeful way. Many who rely on their own shallow inner resources give in to depression, becoming cynical or apathetic.

OUR RIGHTEOUSNESS COMES FROM HIM

Later, we will study Philippians 3:8, where Paul talks about the loss of all things that he had counted as gain, in order that he might gain Christ; and in verse 9:

> *...and may be found in Him, not having a righteousness of my own derived from the Law, but that which is through faith in Christ, the righteousness which comes from God on the basis of faith.*

Whose faith? Our faith in Christ produces righteousness inspired from God.

There are two different items of "molding" righteousness:

(1) God's righteousness—which has the capacity to make us perfect; and

(2) Man's righteousness—which keeps him striving to attain that perfection. [1]

[1] George Covalt

Paul goes on to say that because, through faith, we can become righteous, therefore we can know Christ.

This righteousness is not our own. We cannot become righteous by an act of our own will, especially of that based on law. These "do this and don't do that" rules, so common in the past, will not make us righteous. To become like Christ—"to be found in Him...to know Him and the power of His resurrection, and to share in His sufferings" (Philippians 3:8,9), we need to acknowledge that righteousness necessarily comes from God. We grow in this grace through the guarantee of the Spirit on the basis of our faith.

> *...(so that you may be) filled with the fruits of righteousness which come through Jesus Christ, to the glory and praise of God.*
>
> *—Philippians 1:11*

HE GRANTS UNTO US SONSHIP

> *And He said, "A certain man had two sons; and the younger of them said to his father, 'Father, give me the share of the estate that falls to me.' And he divided his wealth between them.*
>
> *"And not many days later, the younger son gathered everything together and went on a journey into a distant country, and there he squandered his estate with loose living.*
>
> *"Now when he had spent everything, a severe famine occurred in that country, and he began to be in need. And he went and attached himself to one of the citizens of that country, and he sent him into his fields to feed swine. And he was longing to fill his stomach with the pods that the swine were eating, and no one was giving anything to him.*
>
> *"But when he came to his senses, he said, 'How many of my father's hired men have more than enough bread, but I am dying here with hunger! I will get up and go to my father, and will say to him, "Father, I have sinned*

against heaven, and in your sight; I am no longer worthy to be called your son; make me as one of your hired men." '

"And he got up and came to his father. But while he was still a long way off, his father saw him, and felt compassion for him, and ran and embraced him, and kissed him. And the son said to him, 'Father, I have sinned against heaven and in your sight; I am no longer worthy to be called your son.'

"But the father said to his slaves, 'Quickly bring out the best robe and put it on him, and put a ring on his hand and sandals on his feet; and bring the fattened calf, kill it, and let us eat and be merry; for this son of mine was dead, and has come to life again; he was lost, and has been found.' "

—Luke 15:11-24

When the Prodigal Son, realizing at last his lost condition, "came to himself" and finally admitted that his father's hired servants were in a much better position than himself, he considered returning to his father as a hired servant. He counted himself no longer worthy to be called a son.

His father, however, considered him to be a son, and restored unto him sonship. Likewise, our Heavenly Father makes of us sons and daughters, we who possess the mindset of slaves. We do not have the power, the authority, or even the wisdom to be sons, but God has appointed us to be His own. Must we continue to be bound by the "slave mentality"?

So also we, while we were children, were held in bondage under the elemental things of the world. But when the fulness of the time came, God sent forth His Son, born of a woman, born under the Law, in order that He might redeem those who were under the Law, that we might receive the adoption as sons. And because you are sons, God has sent forth the Spirit of His Son into our hearts, crying, "Abba! Father!"

Therefore you are no longer a slave, but a son; and if a son, then an heir through God.

—Galatians 4:3-7

GROWTH AND MOLDING OF THE CHURCH

> *...holding fast to the Head, from whom the whole body, nourished and knit together through its joints and ligaments, grows with a growth that is from God.*
>
> —*Colossians 2:19 (RSV)*

So often church leadership talks in terms of this program or that program, and how many people can be involved, and how many souls *we* will save. Individuals sometimes boast, saying, "I've converted so many souls." This passage in Colossians teaches us, however, that the whole body grows with its growth from God. Yes, we need programs and body activities to give us all opportunities to grow closer. But as the Lord helps us as individuals to grow spiritually because we seek Him, so He will provide the growth of the body as we seek Him together, supporting and loving one another.

FOR NOW

This week, challenge your faith. Step onto the Potter's wheel as a lump of yielding clay by picking up your Bible, reading until you come to one of God's commands or injunctions, and then simply do it. Do not decide, "Well, I don't think that applies to me" or "I'm not smart enough" or "I don't have enough time." Have the faith to take Him at His Word. Be discriminating, of course. If you are a woman, do not try to go to a prison alone. Do not try to teach without preparing your lesson. Do not insist on visiting the sick when a "No Visitors" sign is posted.

But in scriptures such as 2 Timothy 3:15; Matthew 5:14-16; Romans 12; 1 Corinthians 3:16,17, 6:1-8, 6:19,20, and 10:23,24—just to name a few at random—we can immediately have the faith to say, "Yes, Lord; when the writer penned this, that meant that it is good for me; and I, with the help of your Spirit, will make it a part of my life."

Remember that when He gives a command, He bestows on us the ability and affords us the strength to carry it out. Do not limit Him or yourself with a weak faith.

The book of Philippians is filled with direct injunctions to right living, some of which we will be studying. In the meantime:

(1) Rejoice that you do not have to live the Christian life completely by an act of your own will.

(2) Acknowledge the fact that God molds us.

(3) Know that He either is preparing you or has already prepared you for a ministry based on your competence in His kingdom.

(4) Rejoice that you can love with God's love, and that you no longer need to depend exclusively on your own variable feelings to reach out to someone else.

(5) Make every choice in accordance with what you believe God's will to be.

(6) Do what His Word says to do, because you have the faith and the competency to do it (which means, of course, that you must study and meditate on the scriptures in order to know what that Word is).

(7) Appropriate the power of daily prayer in your life. Conscientiously avoid the world's commonest prayer: "Lord, thy will be changed." [2]

But now, O Lord, Thou art our Father; we are the clay, and Thou our Potter;
And all of us are the work of Thy hand.
—*Isaiah 64:8*

Study Questions

(1) Name some things you think (or thought) you can (or could) do for yourself without God's help.

(2) Can you name an event in your life which you think God has used to mold you?

(3) Can you think of a scripture which has changed your life, or at least steered you in a different direction?

(4) Name some "do's and don'ts" which you thought would make you righteous.

(5) Why is it sometimes difficult to love with our brand of love?

[2] William Barclay, *The Gospel of Luke* (Philadelphia, PA: The Westminster Press), pg. 7.

II

The Worst Thing

Paul Stands as an Inspirational Example to Counter That Which We Fear the Most

Text. . . . . Philippians 1:19-26.

Memory Verse. . . . . Philippians 1:21.

Years ago, a speaker asked an audience, "What do you think is the very worst thing that could happen to you? The worst imaginable disruption in your life?" The audience was asked individually to write "the worst thing" down on a piece of paper and keep it in a safe place somewhere. The speaker then proceeded to present a most effective message on Romans 8:35-39—the fact that nothing could separate us from the love of God.

For this listener, then a mother of four small boys, the "very worst thing" was written down as the sudden death of one of the children. I could not imagine anything with which coping could be more difficult, not to say desperate. Several years later, my husband and I did face that exact situation, and we learned firsthand that this promise made by Paul is very real, extremely dynamic, and utterly trustworthy. It is also within this context that our present text becomes quite relevant and lucid.

> *For I know that this shall turn out for my deliverance through your prayers and the provision of the Spirit of Jesus Christ, according to my earnest expectation and hope, that I shall not be put to shame in anything, but that with all boldness, Christ shall even now, as always, be exalted in my body, whether by life or by death.*
>
> *For to me, to live is Christ, and to die is gain.*
>
> *But if I am to live on in the flesh, this will mean fruitful labor for me; and I do not know which to choose.*

> *But I am hard-pressed from both directions, having the desire to depart and be with Christ, for that is very much better; yet to remain on in the flesh is more necessary for your sake. And convinced of this, I know that I shall remain and continue with you all for your progress and joy in the faith, so that your proud confidence in me may bound in Christ Jesus through my coming to you again.*
>
> *—Philippians 1:19-26*

Many cultures today are still enslaved to death. Our missionaries in Africa tell us that in the primitive and naturalistic religions there, people stand in terror of death. They cannot talk about it; there is much mysticism and superstition connected with it; and it is the one greatest fear of their existence. Even Paul, in Romans 5:14, says that death reigned from Adam to Moses. For those who know not God today, in any culture, death reigns supreme.

In Romans 8:6, Paul says that to set the mind on the flesh is death. In the opening chapters of Romans, it is sometimes difficult to determine when Paul is making a distinction between physical death—separation of body from spirit—or spiritual death—separation of the soul from God. Perhaps he is using them interchangeably, or even as one. Certainly, "to set the mind on the flesh" will result in both. But 1 Corinthians 15:54-57 provides proper perspective for this lesson:

> *But when this perishable will have put on the imperishable, and this mortal will have put on immortality, then will come about the saying that is written, "Death is swallowed up in victory.*
>
> *"O death, where is your victory? O death, where is your sting?"*
>
> *The sting of death is sin, and the power of sin is the Law; But thanks be to God, who gives us the victory through our Lord Jesus Christ.*

THE SETTING

Paul was in prison awaiting trial. He had heard, no doubt through the message of Epaphroditus, that there were parties preaching Christ who were not connected with Paul in any way. Because of his chains, more brethren had found the courage to speak out for the Lord in a new and fearlessly energetic way. Some of these brethren were quickened to do this because of their love for Paul and their sympathy for his predicament. But others were motivated by envy and rivalry, and used the occasion of his imprisonment to take advantage of the situation, preaching for their own gain. As Barclay states, "...his imprisonment seemed to present them with a heaven-sent opportunity to advance their own influence and prestige and lessen his" (Barclay, p. 23).

But Paul rejoiced! His great heart was made glad because Christ was preached.

In an earlier case, there was strife over the direction of his ministry.

> *And there arose such a sharp disagreement that they separated from one another, and Barnabus took Mark with him and sailed away to Cyprus. But Paul chose Silas and departed, being committed by the brethren to the grace of the Lord.*
>
> —*Acts 15:39,40*

So even though there was contention, the Lord used this to double His missionary efforts in this case. Paul's imprisonment served even to multiply Christian evangelism there. Too often, rivalries and jealousies mar our participation. If someone else gains a preeminence which we feel should have been ours, we are resentful. Or if another teacher successfully uses innovative methods, we might count him or her as "competition." A theologian might think an evangelist shallow; the evangelist might call the faith of the theologian impractical. Those in a bus ministry might tend to feel that if others are not participating in this program, they are not putting the Lord's best interests in the forefront. Those in a prison ministry might feel resentment if the rest of us fail to give this project personal priority. And on and on the list continues.

But Paul was above all of this. The fact was that Christ being preached was cause for rejoicing, and we should feel the same way. Success in any area of the Lord's work, whether we are involved or not in that particular area, should still evoke enthusiastic rejoicing in our hearts. There was much fervor and activity which Paul was counting as good.

Thus, even in the face of his afflictions, Paul was rejoicing in the preaching of the gospel. A positive, joyous attitude so pervades this apostle's writings that he makes a strong faith look easy. Never once in his epistles does he intimate that the fear of death is a natural phenomenon for the Christian.

THE FEARS OF DEATH

Almost everyone experiences varying degrees of anxiety when facing untried circumstances, places, or people. Accepting a new job, moving to a new city, changing doctors, facing impending surgery, even driving a different car—each encounters hundreds of anxiety-producing situations in a lifetime, all of which are predicated by fear of the unknown. When facing the one great Unknown then, is it any wonder that we exhibit fear?

The unknown factor of *our reactions*, when faced with the death of a loved one, is another legitimate fear. We visualize ourselves reacting one way but, when under stress, our unanticipated emotions may move us in another direction.

Not knowing how to cope is another fear. "How will I get along without him/her?" is a question often asked in the face of death.

Someone has said, "I don't fear death as much as I fear *dying*." This is true. Countless thousands have been taken swiftly and almost painlessly, but countless thousands of others have suffered painful lingering agonies. To be a burden—financially, emotionally, and time-wise—if not a fear, at least is a legitimate dread.

Even Paul, verbally working out his dilemma, stated his preference for "remaining in the flesh"—the Philippians needed him (Philippians 1:24,25). To be needed and loved is what keeps us all young and active. So, *separation from loved ones who need us* is also a legitimate dread.

Separation, of course, is a two-edged sword. We dread a loved one's death because we depend on him or her to fill critical needs in our lives. Often adjustments are made even more complicated because we are seldom aware of the extent of those needs until separation becomes reality. The shock itself is a fear; the adjustments can be traumatic. We all need to search deeply to discover the roles (and properly appreciate them) which loved ones fulfill in our lives.

We fear *leaving a task unfinished.* The Mozarts and Bachs of this world bequeath to us a poignant and relevant legacy: we have gorgeous masterpieces from the pens of each which eternally remain unfinished. More than one idealist has expressed anxiety over leaving this life without making a permanent and significant contribution to the progress of mankind. Leaving our affairs in order and having said all of our good-byes, most of us could depart in peace.

A common tragedy of old age is not that we made good or bad decisions, but that we *failed to make the most of our "now" times:* we took our mates for granted; we voiced too many words of criticism, and too few of encouragement, uplifting thoughts, praise, and appreciation; we failed to rejoice in present blessings due to worry about the cessation of future ones. Our conversation becomes punctuated with "If only I had ____________," "Why didn't I do/say ____________," and "I wish I had ____________."

The negative, the stressful, and the burdensome intruded so into our glorious "now" that we, however inadvertently, blocked most of the peace and joy messages which radiate continually to us from God's presence.

Perhaps the consummate fear of death comes from the anticipation of the *Judgment.* Even though some anticipate "going to Heaven when they die," they do not yet know the Lord God as Father. Meeting such an awesome Personage as a stranger is indeed a fearsome proposition. This is one of the elements in the "fear of the unknown." Knowledge of God—His plan, His Son, His way for your life and your eternity—can certainly ease or erase entirely the fear of judgment.

> *It is a terrifying thing to fall into the hands of the living God.* *Hebrews 10:31.*

PAUL'S PERSPECTIVE OF DEATH

Paul must have asked himself inwardly, "How can I rejoice, when I am sitting here awaiting a trial which will determine whether I live or die?" But Paul had already faced death many times before. He knew that death could not separate him from Christ.

> *For to me, to live is Christ, and to die is gain.*

This verse reveals Paul's intimate walk and friendship with Christ and represents the perspective of the entire book of Philippians from

Paul's standpoint. It shows his relationship with Christ as Elder Brother. We can almost feel Christ saying to Paul, "You know, Little Brother, if you have seen and have known me, you know our Dad, too." The whole epistle is colored with Paul's life-view as pictured in this verse.

In our text for this chapter, Paul only discusses one choice which he has. It was not whether he wanted to be in prison or to be released. The Gospel was being preached anyway. It was not necessarily whether to go to the Philippians or to stay; he merely encourages them to "stand firm in one spirit, with one mind striving side by side for the faith of the Gospel, and not frightened in anything by your opponents" (Philippians 1:27,28). His choice certainly was not whether to live with or without Christ. That had been decided.

He merely seemed to be in a dilemma about whether he would prefer to live or die, knowing with no doubt at all that either would be "with full courage" (Philippians 1:20, RSV). When we have this perspective, according to Ralph Herring, we are in a " 'heads I win, tails you lose' position in reference to anything Satan can do. In either case, Paul stood to win" (Herring, p. 58).

WHAT WAS CHRIST TO PAUL?

For Paul, living was Christ. Christ, for Paul at his baptism, had been the beginning of life (Acts 9:18). Christ had been the continuing of life (Acts 18:9,10). And Christ was the end of life, for it is toward Him and His presence for eternity that life leads.

Can we afford to make Him anything less today? The question was asked recently, "Why don't Christians pray more?" Of course, the answers finally must rest with each Christian; but certainly one of the fundamental reasons is that we do not understand the full implications of eternity—either for ourselves or for others.

Christ was Paul's inspiration, his task, his strength, and his reward. Correlating all of Paul's writings, we do no injustice to say that he might have made this statement:

> *I have no secrets from Christ, no locked doors from any part of my life from Him. I have no part to which I am not entirely committed to Christ, no part which He does not control.*
>
> *—Robertson, p. 94*

WHAT WAS DEATH TO PAUL?

To Paul, death, the physical separation, meant simply more of Christ. All that death could do would be simply to give him more of what it is to be in Christ and with Christ (see Philippians 3:8). Of course, Paul's ultimate choice for himself is left to God; but he verbally works out his own dilemma by concluding that, on behalf of the Philippians, it would be more profitable for him to stay on in the flesh (Philippians 1:24). And, having decided this, he was convinced that he would come to them again (Philippians 1:26). Perhaps he was indeed able (see 1 Timothy 1:3). His coming to them would have given them one more reason to glory in the Lord. On the other hand, the converse would not have given them a reason to feel ashamed. In Paul's flowing statement of a triumphant death, "the Philippians could look at Paul and see in him a shining example of how, through Christ, a man can face the worst erect and unafraid" (Barclay, p. 28, 29).

THE GOOD NEWS

The release from the powers of death as though it did not exist is one of the most salient points of the Gospel which we preach, if not the most. We need to realize that our deaths in the Lord's sight are precious (Psalm 116:15). My death marks an end to my struggles, trials, and miseries; but most of all, in Christ, it marks the cessation of all that can separate me from God (Isaiah 59:1,2).

Let us hence no longer regard death as a dread separation of body and soul, but as a welcome reunion with all we hold dearest.

Study Questions

(1) For you, what is the "worst thing" that can happen?

(2) How did Paul view death?

(3) Name some things that Christ meant to Paul (see Acts 9:15-19, 18:9,10; 2 Corinthians 12:9; Philippians 1:23, 3:8).

(4) Euripides, the Greek philosopher, said, "Who knows if living is indeed dying, while dying is living?" What do you think he meant?

(5) Is Paul teaching that it would be better if we just all died?

(6) What verse or phrase shows Paul's great love for the Philippians?

(7) What did Paul mean in Philippians 2:17 when he said that he would rejoice even if he were "poured out as a drink offering upon the sacrifice and service of their faith?"

III

A Manner Worthy

Paul Enjoins the Philippians to Live in "A Manner Worthy" of the Gospel of Christ

Text. . . . . Philippians 1:27-2:4.

Supplementary. . . . . Philippians 3:20, 4:2,3.

Memory Verse . . . . . Philippians 1:27.

The letters that were sent from the pen of the Apostle Paul, both to churches and to individuals, very generally follow similar formats. The first part of the book usually deals with the deep theological themes of the New Testament: man's fallen state, God's plan of reconciliation, the relationship of the Old Law to the New, the respective relationships between grace, law, faith, works, and love, etc.

The second part of the book is more often devoted toward educating his readers to live in such a way that the Gospel, God, Christ, and the Holy Spirit are glorified.

It is certainly beyond the scope of this lesson to detail every event in Christ's life in which He acted with grace, wisdom, and discretion; in other words, in a manner worthy of His mission. Nor is it within this framework to document the lives, lived in a worthy manner, of the apostles and their key followers. The book of James eloquently delineates what to most of us represents "a manner worthy." But we are going to look in this lesson at what Paul possibly meant when he used this language.

LIVE IN A MANNER WORTHY

Only conduct yourselves in a manner worthy of the gospel of Christ; so that whether I come and see you or remain absent, I may hear of you that you are standing firm in one spirit, with one mind striving together for the faith of the gospel; in no way alarmed by your opponents—which is a sign of destruction for them, but of salvation for you, and that too, from God.

For to you it has been granted for Christ's sake, not only to believe in Him, but also to suffer for His sake, experiencing the same conflict which you saw in me, and now hear to be in me.

If therefore there is any encouragement in Christ, if there is any consolation of love, if there is any fellowship of the Spirit, if any affection and compassion, make my joy complete by being of the same mind, maintaining the same love, united in spirit, intent on one purpose.

Do nothing from selfishness or empty conceit, but with humility of mind let each of you regard one another as more important than himself; do not merely look out for your own personal interests, but also for the interests of others.

—Philippians 1:27-2:4

The verb which is translated in Philippians 1:27 to "*live* in a manner *worthy" of the gospel is* πολιτεύεσθε (polituesthe) and means "to order one's life and conduct in a certain manner as to habits and principles." It is a verb which gets its root from πόλις (polis), a Greek word which means "a city; an enclosed and walled town; the inhabitants of that city."

Established in 357 B.C. by Philip of Macedon, Philippi was now a Roman colony. In Acts 16:12, we are told that it was "the leading city of the district of Macedonia"; so, as such, one might liken it to one of our state capitals. It had a contingent of Roman troops stationed there, and its citizens possessed a civic pride nurtured from being under the government of Rome. Civic responsibility ran high.

So Paul is appealing to this awareness by using this word which means "citizenship." One properly could translate the first part of verse 27 as saying "Only let your manner of life be fitting as citizens of the kingdom of the gospel of Christ." This appeal is strengthened by his use of this same word in Philippians 3:20, when he tells the Philippians and us, too, that "our citizenship is in Heaven." By using this word, Paul is saying:

> *You and I know full well the privileges and responsibilities of being a Roman citizen. You know full well how, even in Philippi, so many miles from Rome, you must still live and act as a Roman does. Well then, remember that you have an even higher duty than that. Wherever you are, you must live as befits a citizen of the Kingdom of God.*
>
> *—Barclay, p. 30*

So what does he go on to tell them in the remainder of Chapter One?

(1) Stand fast.

(2) Be united.

(3) Be unconquerable.

(4) Have a cool, calm courage.

Before we go on in Philippians, let us examine similar language in Ephesians.

> *I, therefore, the prisoner of the Lord, entreat you* to walk *in a manner worthy of the calling with which you have been called, with all humility and gentleness, with patience, showing forbearance to one another in love, being diligent to preserve the unity of the Spirit in the bond of peace.*
>
> *There is one body and one Spirit, just as also you were called in one hope of your calling; one Lord, one faith, one baptism, one God and Father of all who is over all and through all and in all.*
>
> *—Ephesians 4:1-6*

In verse one, describing the life we are to lead, Paul uses a different word: περιπατεῖν (peripatein); literally, "to walk about." Here, it means "to maintain a certain quality or walk of life." This verse we also usually associate with living worthily.

How are we to do this, Paul? In Ephesians 4:2:

(1) Be completely humble and gentle.

(2) Be patient.

(3) Bear with one another in love.

What did he say in Philippians 2:1-4?

(1) Be affectionate and compassionate.

(2) Be humble.

(3) Consider others better than yourselves.

(4) Care for the interests of others.

But his great plea in each of these passages is that for unity. The worthy manner of life—both aspects of it, both references—is shown to the world by our unity, and this is brought about by those things listed above.

In the last part of Philippians 1:27, Paul tells them that whether he gets to see them or only hear about them, he has confidence in their unity "without being frightened in any way by those who oppose you. Christian unity, then, is a trademark of our salvation! And from Philippians 2:2:

> *Make my joy complete by being of the same mind, maintaining the same love, united in spirit, intent on one purpose.*

(1) The same mind: an internal and personal unity.

(2) Maintaining the same love: a unity between these persons.

(3) United in spirit: souls bound together by like attitudes.

(4) United in purpose: one entity moving toward a common goal.

The reasons he gives for unity in Ephesians are equally as desirable.

> *And He gave some as apostles, and some as prophets, and some as evangelists, and some as pastors and teachers, for the equipping of the saints for the work of service, to the building up of the body of Christ; until we all attain to the unity of the faith, and of the knowledge of the Son of God, to a mature man, to the measure of the stature which belongs to the fulness of Christ.*
>
> *As a result, we are no longer to be children, tossed here and there by waves, and carried about by every wind of doctrine, by the trickery of men, by craftiness in deceitful scheming; but speaking the truth in love, we are to grow up in all aspects into Him, who is the head, even Christ, from whom the whole body, being fitted and held together by that which every joint supplies, according to the proper working of each individual part, causes the growth of the body for the building up of itself in love.*
>
> —*Ephesians 4:11-16*

THE PURPOSE OF OUR GIFTS

The reason for each one of the many gifts given to each of us is to build us all up into the unity of faith and knowledge, and to maturity, so that we will not be drawn away at every peculiarity of doctrine which comes along. Calvin, in his commentary on Ephesians 4:11-16, states that no Christian is so gifted but what he needs the gifts of others to help him reach Heaven.

One's weaknesses are upheld and overcome by another's strengths. No office is too glorious that it can be sufficiently independent of the others, or that it can singlehandedly uphold "lesser" functions. There is no worthy undertaking authorized to be done by one function to the disuse of others—no activity by proxy. No station is so base that its malfunction can go unfelt.

The purpose of the gifts, then, is to lead to unity of the faith and a knowledge of Jesus. The purpose of this unity is to lead us into maturity, wholeness, and completeness so that we may not be like unstable, purposeless, and undirected children. The purpose of this maturity, then, is the ultimate growth of the Body into the Head.

WHAT IS UNITY?

One can almost hear some Christian brother saying, "Oh, no; not me. I'm not going to believe that my walking 'in a worthy manner' has anything to do with my brothers and sisters. I'm going to be as good as I can, do as much good as I can, and be as close to God as I can, and get to Heaven. If they don't want to live in a unified manner, that's their problem." This brother, of course, has "I" problems. Too often our idea of unity is: "If we agree and understand some theological concept alike, we are united; unless everyone else agrees with us, they are wrong."

Brethren, this is a striving for union, not unity. Not even all the apostles saw everything alike. We need to yearn for, and to build, bridges, not walls. We need sincere, open-minded, prayerful study of scripture to know what is God's will; then to strive carefully not to impose anything on others which God does not impose on us or them.

In his first epistle, John wrote some words characteristic of unity:

> *But if we walk in the light as He Himself is in the light, we have fellowship with one another, and the blood of Jesus His Son cleanses us from all sin.*
>
> —*1 John 1:7*

> *We know that we have passed out of death into life, because we love the brethren. He who does not love abides in death.*
>
> —*1 John 3:14*

> *And the one who keeps His commandments abides in Him, and He in him. And we know by this that He abides in us, by the Spirit which He has given us.*
>
> —*1 John 3:24*

The spirit of unity is conceived and born because of the love we have for each other as individuals, for God, Christ, and the Holy Spirit, for the church collectively, and for the Word. When any one of these is attacked by forces without, we draw together and are made strong; if attacked from within, our unity is endangered to the core.

As the church moved farther down the time line, away from her primitive but inspired origins, Paul could see the seeds of disunity being sown at every juncture. Individuals were taking their God-given, powerful, and dynamic gifts, and were appropriating them for personal gain.

THE NEGATIVE IN PHILIPPIANS

In this letter, the only negative note—the only hint of even a warning—issues from the threat of division. This letter, so full of joy, love, and hope, has been called Paul's "love letter." But the seeds of discord constantly undermine the text.

Speaking in the first chapter (Philippians 1:15-17), Paul mentions that some preach Christ out of envy, rivalry, and partisanship in order to advance their own gains. This dissension sprung from *wrong motives* for preaching Christ—Christians preaching to advance themselves, and likely their own pet causes.

In Philippians 3:2, Paul issues a warning against "the dogs, the evilworkers...those who mutilate the flesh." Most commentators consider these to be Judaizers who would rend the Body by imposing again the ordinances of Judaism. This condemnation could apply today to any who would preach *false doctrines* and, again, the disorder comes from supposed Christians.

In Philippians 3:17-19, Paul warns them not to imitate the earthly-minded "many," for they "live as enemies of the cross of Christ. Their end is destruction, their God is the belly, and they glory in their shame, with minds set on earthly things." This came as an exhortation against *worldliness*. These probably were from pagan influences which crept inside the body. There were those who had embraced Christianity nominally who continued to live as enemies of the Cross. Paul often shed tears over his worries for these in the Church (2 Corinthians 2:4).

In Philippians 4:2, Paul exhorts two women, apparently both preeminent in the Philippian church, "to agree in the Lord." They had "labored side by side (with Paul) in the Gospel"—hard workers, respected, talented women, probably laboring from noble motives, but who probably were divided by a spirit of envy and jealousy.

CAUSES OF DISUNITY

> *Do nothing from selfishness or conceit, but in humility count others better than yourselves. Let each of you look not only to his own interests, but also to the interests of others.*
>
> *—Philippians 2:3,4 (RSV)*

Barclay finds three great causes for disunity in these two verses. All of them, really, arise from selfishness.

(1) Selfish ambition. *People work, not to advance Christ, but to advance themselves.*

(2) Vain conceit *(empty glorying).*

> *Prestige is for many people an even greater temptation than wealth. To be admired and respected, to have a platform seat, to have one's opinion sought, to be known by name and appearance, even to be flattered, are for many people most desirable things.*
>
> *—Barclay, p. 32*

The aim of the Christian should be to glorify God—to show *His* power, grace, and majesty, rather than his own.

(3) Concentration on self. *If a man is forever concerned first and foremost with his own interests, he is bound to collide with others. "I've got to win this, or to have that" means that whatever is beneficial for the Body must take second place. What does this do to unity?*

A PLEA FOR UNITY

Paul's appeal in Philippians 1:27-30 can be likened, and is in the Greek, to a pair of scales. In our last lesson, he measured one possibility against another—that of living or dying. In this one, in the word translated "worthy," the picture occurs again.

On a pair of scales, of course, an accepted standard of measurement was used to determine the weight of the substance against which it was matched. The "worth" was found as the standard weight drew or led the beam to a horizontal balance. So the privileges available to us in the Gospel must be matched by our responsibilities as Christian citizens. The Gospel provides us with great freedom. The manner in which we balance freedom with responsibility is the standard by which we measure our own weight of worth. The exhortation is that we should strive to live in such an exemplary way that we balance the weight of the gifts and privileges bestowed. A Christian will never match his worth to God's gifts, but he should adopt this lofty ambition.

Their "worthy manner" was to be marked by a striving together (contending: NIV), not unlike those of trained and disciplined athletes. Just as they were, so are we to train, to practice, to work as a team, to *strain* together toward a common goal. This appeal in Philippians 1:27f is to a life that matches the glorious destiny of Heaven. The quality of their daily living was Paul's great concern here, and this quality was notably marked by their unity.

There should be a spirit in every local church which finds all together in Christ, straining as one "for the faith of the Gospel" (Philippians 1:27), so that "when each...is working properly, makes bodily growth and upbuilds itself in love" (Ephesians 4:16b).

Study Questions

(1) Describe in your own words what "living in a worthy manner" means to you. Name some favorite scriptures to strengthen this viewpoint.

(2) What was the greatest danger confronting the Philippian church? (See Philippians 1:27, 2:1-4, 3:2, 4:2,3.)

(3) Read also Ephesians 4:1-6 in conjunction with Philippians 1:27 and 2:1,2. In the context of these verses, what does Paul say that "a worthy manner" is?

(4) As you read Philippians 1:29, ask yourself if you consider suffering to be a privilege. Review Philippians 1:12-18 to find truths to help you rejoice in the midst of tribulation. List these.

(5) From Philippians 2:3,4, Barclay lists three great causes for disunity (quoted in this text); discuss. Are there any others?

(6) List several negative results, either using biblical references or taken from your own observation, which occur when disunity prevails. Are there any positive results?

IV

The Quickening Power of Love

Love Should Be the Motivating Force of Every Action Within Our Christian Fellowship

Text.............. *Philippians 2:1-4.*

Supplementary..... *Philippians 1:3-5, 7-11; 4:10, 14-20.*

Memory Verse..... *Philippians 2:1,2.*

As was mentioned in the last lesson, the book of Philippians has been called the "love letter" of the New Testament. It is the only one of Paul's letters which contains minimal chastisement and rebuke. To read it, one becomes aware of the great affection Paul holds for the Philippians, that which they hold for him, and the bonds of love and integrity between Paul, Timothy, Epaphroditus, and the Philippians.

Likewise, Paul's opening remarks in Chapter 1:3-5 reflect an outpouring of thanksgiving, joy, and caring. Verses 7 and 8 of the same mention their complete and intimate participation with Paul in his imprisonment, in his spiritual involvement, and in his ministry of evangelism. Verses 9 through 11 embrace his prayer for the Philippians:

> *And this I pray, that your love may abound still more and more in real knowledge and all discernment, so that you may approve the things that are excellent, in order to be sincere and blameless until the day of Christ; having been filled with the fruit of righteousness which comes through Jesus Christ, to the glory and praise of God.*

It remains an amazing question—why did Paul not say that the Philippians simply needed knowledge or wisdom in order to approve the things that are excellent? Why was he praying that their *love* might abound more and more in order to accomplish these things? This hearkens back to 1 Corinthians 13, of course; without love, their knowledge of all things excellent, their sincerity, and blamelessness would prove unfruitful, reducing their religion to Pharisaical observance.

Always pray this prayer for one another! If this were to be fulfilled in our lives, to borrow a phrase, "all these other things will be added unto you!"

In Chapter 4, Paul again expresses his abundant gratitude for their support and concern. In 4:14-20, he pours out his feelings of gratitude, thanksgiving, and affection for the material, emotional, and spiritual support which the Philippians had lavished upon him.

Each of us who possess any degree of conscience whatever has a sense of "oughtness"—a sense of duty—to accomplish those goals or tasks which are ours, even perhaps with something less than enthusiasm. But Paul's love and that of the Philippians motivated them far above the level of "we should" to the lofty heights of "may we?"

In our last lesson, we discussed some causes of division. In this, let us look at some methods for healing. In Chapter 2:1,2, Paul pens a semi-mini-sermon on how to restore unity. Appealing to all within them which is characteristic of their pervading Christlikeness, he begins.

WORDS TO HEAL

> *If therefore there is any encouragement in Christ, if there is any consolation of love, if there is any fellowship of the Spirit, if any affection and compassion, (2) make my joy complete by being of the same mind, maintaining the same love, united in spirit, intent on one purpose.*

(1) "If therefore there is any *encouragement* in Christ..."—This word in Greek is παράκλησις (paraklasis), and is synonymous with exhortation, solace, comfort, consolation, cheering, and supporting. In the masculine form, it is often used to refer to the Holy Spirit and His work. Here, then,

this encouragement could originate through the Holy Spirit, because we are "in Christ" and have been promised the indwelling measure of the Holy Spirit. However, because we are "in Christ," Paul could mean that this comforting exists, or should exist, between members of Christ's body. At any rate, Paul uses a first-class condition in Greek which precludes the statement to be true. Thus, the "if" with all of these statements is an attention-getting rhetorical device, and carries the idea of "since" or "because."

A word of encouragement—it is never out of place, almost always needed, and invariably welcome. The exhortation, solace, comfort, consolation, cheering, and supporting, available because we are in Christ, whether from the Holy Spirit directly or from the Spirit through the brethren, is not a force to be taken lightly. Coupled with love, comforting, consoling, cheering, and supporting can create an unbreakable bond between brethren. Oh, that the church were possessed of more Barnabases, one whose name means "Son of Encouragement." The impulse to encourage is quickened by love; when enveloped in love, the word of encouragement becomes itself a quickening action.

(2) "...if there is any *consolation* of love..."—This word translated "consolation" is παραμύθιον (paramutheion). Moulton defines this as "gentle cheering; encouragement; tender persuasion" ("incentive;" RSV). It is always bound up with paraklasis, but denotes the comfort granted in this present sphere—God's comfort channeled through human vessels. Characterized by the word fitly spoken, it means a gentle squeeze, a warm smile, and a soft shoulder to cry on. This consolation (or incentive) of love can give stability to stumbling feet and strength to weary hands.

(3) "...if there is any *fellowship* of the Spirit..."—The Greek word, translated in the RSV as "participation," is κοινωνία (koinonia), and means "fellowship, partnership, and that which is shared." The "bare bones" Greek literally says, "if there is any fellowship of spirit..." or "spiritual fellowship." Thus, by eliminating the definite article, Paul seems to imply the sharing and commonality of spirit which we possess in Christ but not directly relating to the Holy

Spirit himself; i.e., "They possess a spirit of enthusiasm in that congregation." However, almost every translation consulted yielded the translation, "If any fellowship of (or "with") *the* Spirit..."

So whether we have in common the sharing cemented by the Holy Spirit or merely hold in common a like spirit among ourselves, Paul counts this as a powerful motivation for unity. Indeed, a true Christian spirit of fellowship and love is spawned by the Holy Spirit, in the presence of which arguing and dissident behavior vanish.

(4) "...if any *affection*..."—The Greek σπλάγχνα (splagkna); literally, the bowels or viscera. The Greeks considered this area of the body to be the seat of the tenderest affections and gentlest mercies; hence, the many and varied translations available to us. It is the seat of mercy, sympathy, and compassion of the tenderest and most involved kind.

(5) "...and *compassion*..."—The Greek οἰκτιρμοί (oiktiermoi); Moulton: kindness in relieving sorrow and want. If the word above was the seat of compassion, so this word is the compassion itself.

These last two words summarize the first three phrases, consolidating them all into one great plea.

PAUL'S PLEA

He has marshaled his strongest vocabulary guns to say that, since there is available to us within the total framework of Christianity...

(1) Comfort and support from the Holy Spirit, in and through Christ;

(2) Incentive and consolation because of the love of God; and

(3) Fellowship and participation in and through the Holy Spirit;

...it is therefore possible to find and nurture these qualities between brethren, all because of God-spawned love. Because we have these things in fellowship with the Godhead, we can and should behave the same way to each other.

The church, although made up of human beings, is more than the sum of her parts. Because we are Christ's body, the Holy Spirit becomes our soul. As we grow in love—in comfort, support, consolation, and fellowship—we can love the unlovable, strengthen the weak, lift up the fallen, and calm the unruly, all with a dynamic energy which belies our own abilities to do so. God never tells us in the New Testament that our problems will cease when we become Christians, but He does tell us that we will have the power to live triumphantly. He gives no command or injunction that does not bear with it the empowering ability to carry it out. The unity which today seems so elusive is indeed possible when each one relinquishes the almighty Self and becomes his own working part of Christ's Body, personifying the servant mentality (see Chapter V).

Paul's use of the words in Philippians 2:1 translated "affection" and "compassion" carries with it the idea of all that is genuine in the Christian experience. THESE THINGS ARE THE SUMMATION AND SUBSTANCE OF CHRISTIAN FELLOWSHIP. They represent Christian commitment of the most complete and fundamental stamp. They reveal the evidence of God's grace and man's response to it which summarize the Lord's injunction to "love thy neighbor as thyself." They show the immediacy of our fellowship with Christ, and flood our being with the warmth of His love. The Greek words for "tenderness and compassion" bear a flood of genuineness and deep personal involvement which grip and profoundly move the whole man, possible only in Christ.

Having thus described the real embodiment of the Christian life, he pleads with them to "be of the same mind; have the same love; be in full accord and of one mind" (Philippians 2:2).

> *Do nothing from selfishness or empty conceit, but with humility of mind let each of you regard one another as more important than himself. Do not merely look out for your own personal interests, but also for the interests of others.*
>
> *—Philippians 2:3,4*

The presence of love is indicated in verses one and two; its work is outlined in verses three and four. The things Paul mentions in the latter—base self-seeking, empty conceit, and selfish interests—are all common symptoms of selfishness to be countered by humility, an allegiance to a higher ideal, preference for others, and the servant mindset.

If Paul could see the church today, how his great heart would grieve at the dissension and wrangling among us! He has shown us what corrective measures are available to us—first from God, then Christ, and now the Holy Spirit—encouragement, consolation, fellowship, solace, comfort, cheering, support, incentive, tender persuasion, partnership, mercy, sympathy, compassion, and kindness—all bound up in one word, really—LOVE!

THE QUICKENING POWER OF LOVE

The answer to unity is love. If one possesses the love of Christ, he will do nothing out of base self-seeking, or be motivated by selfish conceit; but in humility, he will consider others better than himself, and be willing to look after their interests.

The church today is plagued by disunity. Some tear the Body of Christ at the least pretext—often by Pharisaical wrangling over a scripture, sometimes taken out of context, misused, and misapplied. So very often a man, in his pride, will "find a new truth" in a passage, and will then split congregations in an effort to enforce his opinion on his brethren. Ralph Herring, in his commentary, states a corollary to this idea:

> *The differences which so often mar our fellowship are attributable more to an unwillingness to see the problem from another's viewpoint than from difficulties in the problem itself.*
>
> *Herring, p. 66*

The sins of the flesh will mean condemnation for the world, but the sins of attitude will be the undoing of many in the church. A man, with God's help, can correct and rise above the sins of the flesh; but it takes God, with willingness from man, to cleanse the deep recesses of the heart.

The threat of disunity was continuous in Paul's day. The Philippian church was plagued by the threat of division and apostasy by Judaizing teachers (see Philippians 3:2, 17-19). The various factors of pride, envy, rivalry, and rebellion entered in.

Paul would not have written these things had the Philippians not needed them. He used their weaknesses to point the way for us—we who are also ever struggling toward the spirit of unity. Someone has said that "the church is not a place for perfect people," but we might wish to add that it *is* a perfect place for people.

To implement unity in our lives and in our churches:

(1) Pray! Pray for the spirits of encouragement, consolation, love, and the other traits mentioned, to hold sway in your own life.

(2) Watch for opportunities to console and encourage.

(3) Pray for God to stretch your own capacity for loving, to love with *His* gracious, pure, unbounded love.

(4) Look for ways to build up the Body, but be careful of your own motives. Seek to glorify Christ, and surrender your talents to God. He gave them for the building up of the Body. Relinquish your "right" to direct them yourself, and let the Holy Spirit fit them, under His direction, into your local congregation. God will be glorified; your congregation will be blessed; and you will be justifiably exalted by the Lord, not shamefully so by your own efforts (see James 4:10; 2 Peter 5:6).

(5) This week, take an interest in a more timid member of your congregation. Find out about his/her hobbies and projects outside the usual church activities.

(6) Practice each of these words and their concepts as you understand them in your life, at your level of spirituality right now. You and your congregation cannot help but grow into closer unity.

Study Questions

(1) The book of Philippians has been called "the love letter" of the New Testament. Can you guess why?

(2) What does love do for a task at hand?

(3) Name some synonyms for "encouragement." Can you find other scriptures which talk about encouragement?

(4) Who was "the Son of Encouragement"? Why?

(5) What did Paul mean by "...fellowship in the Spirit..." in Philippians 2:1?

(6) What characteristics of love did Paul leave out in Philippians 2:1?

(7) Does he mean that these characteristics are from the Godhead or that they come because of interpersonal relationships in the Body?

(8) Is this really all we need to promote unity in the body?

(9) What other evidences of "the quickening power of love" do we find in Philippians (i.e., what did the Philippians' love for Paul motivate them to do)? See Philippians 1:7 and 4:10,14-20.

(10) According to Philippians 1:9-11, what else will love enable us to do?

V

The Mind of Christ

Paul Presents the Ultimate Basis for Unity— The Example of Christ Jesus Himself

Text. . . . . Philippians 2:5-11.

Memory Verse. . . . . Philippians 2:9-11.

In the past two lessons, we have studied some of the causes and some of the cures of disunity. To counteract this greatest threat to the Philippian church, Paul has been pleading with them to live in harmony, to lay aside their personal ambitions, their desire for prominence, and their individual pride, and to bear in their hearts the selfless desire to serve. His ultimate appeal is to point to the zenith of the faith—the Lord Himself.

> *Have this attitude in yourselves which was also in Christ Jesus, who, although He existed in the form of God, did not regard equality with God a thing to be grasped, but emptied Himself, taking the form of a bond-servant, and being made in the likeness of men. And being found in appearance as a man, He humbled Himself by becoming obedient to the point of death, even death on a cross.*
>
> *Therefore also God highly exalted Him, and bestowed on Him the name which is above every name, that at the name of Jesus every knee should bow, of those who are in heaven, and on earth, and under the earth, and that every tongue should confess that Jesus Christ is Lord, to the glory of God the Father.*
>
> *—Philippians 2:5-11*

Few passages in the entire Bible are able to acquaint us with Christ's nature with more elegance, grace, simplicity, and intimacy than does this brief passage. It is a powerful statement on the deity of Christ, of His humanity, His mission, and His accomplishment. Concerning the considerations of theology, it is the most profound statement in the book of Philippians. It presents at once the deepest and most exalting enigma surrounding Christ Himself—that of His God/Man essence, and the most simple and humbling example which He brought to mankind—strength in being a servant.

We can attain a fuller understanding of this passage if we examine a few words from the Greek first.

THE FORM OF GOD

> *Have this attitude in yourselves which was also in Christ Jesus, who, although He existed in the* form *of God...*

> *μορφῆ (morphe: form): the form proper to a being; individual appearance as it truly is; the whole, in and for itself; essence, existence, or being; that which corresponds with reality.*

Morphe is fundamental and must exist in some form. When once adopted, it always keeps to the same form. It is the permanent expression of existence. This form, which was therefore the essence of Christ, ascribes to Him the essential attributes of God, the characteristics of deity.

> *And He is the image of the invisible God, the first-born of all creation. For by Him all things were created, both in the heavens and on earth, visible and invisible, whether thrones or dominions or rulers or authorities—all things have been created by Him and for Him. And He is before all things, and in Him all things hold together. He is also head of the body, the church; and He is the beginning, the first-born from the dead; so that He Himself might come to have first place in everything. For it was the Father's good pleasure for all the*

fulness to dwell in Him, and through Him to reconcile all things to Himself, having made peace through the blood of His cross; through Him, I say, whether things on earth or things in Heaven.

—Colossians 1:15-20

And He is the radiance of His glory and the exact representation of His nature, and upholds all things by the word of His power. When He had made purification of sins, He sat down at the right hand of the Majesty on High; having become as much better than the angels, as He has inherited a more excellent name than they.

—Hebrews 1:3,4

BUT EMPTIED HIMSELF

"...did not count equality with God a thing to be grasped, but emptied *Himself..."*

One of the great theological debates of Christendom concerns the "emptying" of Christ to become a slave. Did He divest Himself of all of His God-like form? Did He limit His knowledge and actions in order to be Man? Which attributes of God did He give up? Or did He keep only a finite measure of all of them?

The study and debate over the doctrine of kenosis (from the Greek κενόω: I empty) is usually waged along the lines of the personal convictions of the debater. Some, seeking to "prove" Jesus only a man, state that by completely emptying Himself, He discarded all attributes of deity, was totally a man here on this earth and throughout His ministry, and became God again only when His soul returned to God at His death on the cross.

Others, seeking to explain His exemplary life, His ability to resist temptation, and His perfect expertise in dealing with people, assert that He only emptied Himself of the privilege of remaining with the Father, retaining all other trappings of deity. Touching on some of the tenets of gnosticism, this doctrine has led some to say that He was God to such an extent that He did not have a real body, but only appeared to be a man, did not really suffer all the agonies of the crucifixion, and was able to withstand temptation because He was God, not being tempted like a man.

Both extremes strip Jesus of the credibility He claimed for Himself as the Son of God and the Son of Man. The magnitude and direction of the debaters seem to depend on what the declaimer wishes to prove.

However, the key lies in several scriptures from John 5:

> *Jesus therefore answered and was saying to them, "Truly, truly, I say to you, the Son can do nothing of Himself, unless it is something He sees the Father doing; for whatever the Father does, these things the Son also does in like manner. For the Father loves the Son and shows Him all things that He Himself is doing; and greater works than these will He show Him, that you may marvel. For just as the Father raises the dead and gives them life, even so the Son also gives life to whom He wishes. For not even the Father judges any one, but He has given all judgment to the Son, in order that all may honor the Son, even as they honor the Father who sent Him...For just as the Father has life in Himself, even so He gave to the Son also to have life in Himself; and He gave Him authority to execute judgment, because He is the Son of Man...I can do nothing on My own initiative. As I hear, I judge; and My judgment is just, because I do not seek My own will, but the will of Him who sent Me...But the witness which I have is greater than that of John; for the works which the Father has given Me to accomplish, the very works that I do, bear witness of Me, that the Father has sent Me... I have come in my Father's name...*
>
> *—John 5:19-23, 26,27, 30, 36, 43a*

There is, therefore, the very real probability that Jesus, emptying Himself voluntarily, was being refilled at each step in His earthly walk according to the Father's Master Plan, as the Father revealed to Jesus His Will, His Words, and His Power.

As with so very many things in the Bible, why must we, as finite human beings, find a compelling need to explain an act of deity in order to accept it? Where is our faith? One of the most glorious facts of Christianity remains that Christ came to us, completely God, out of an infinite love, of which we can only comprehend a miniscule portion (if indeed it can even be "apportioned"). He emptied Himself of all that was Heaven, all that it meant to be in the exalted Presence of the Father, and all that being in a pure, holy, sinless, griefless, and pristine Paradise meant. He, because of this love, and because He, being deity, understood the consequences of the alternative, voluntarily divested Himself (of what and to what extent we simply cannot be precise) and took on the form—not just the outward appearance, but the real, unchangeable, and essential nature—of a slave. If He had been so human-like that, 2,000 years after the fact, any one of us could say precisely how and in what amount Christ was God and in what manner He was Man, then He would not be enough God to handle each of our problems. Someone within our midst would be able to understand Him completely. Man must have a God bigger than that! Why do we dare question? By doing so, we do not diminish Him in the least, except in our own eyes.

> *"He was God enough to meet every possible need of man, and Man enough to fulfill every requirement for the sacrificial Lamb of God."*
>
> *—Unknown*

While maintaining His God-likeness, His acute sensitivity and awareness of sin, and His empathy and compassion for each one of us miserable, sin-filled human beings, He became God's, and hence our, slave—His will completely submitted to God's. Because of infinite agape love, His will also was completely submitted to *our* own best interests.

THE FORM OF A SLAVE

> *"...but emptied Himself, taking the* form *of a* bond-servant*..."*

The Greek word δοῦλος (doulos), translated in the RSV as "servant," is better rendered as "slave," for μίσθιος (misthios) is Greek for "paid servant" or "hireling." "Doulos" is designated as one being completely submitted to the will, even the whim, of another. So Christ went from all of the essential nature of God; and retaining this, He also assumed the essential nature of a slave, not merely in outward form, but that which is retained in the very inner being.

THE LIKENESS OF MAN

"...and being made in the likeness *of men..."*

> *ὁμοίωμα (homoioma: likeness): that which has been made after the likeness of something; a figure, image, likeness, reproduction; representation; what is made similar, a copy; synonymous with εἰκών (eikon). It always has the concrete sense of "copy."*

In other words, Jesus was "being born in a copy of mankind." He looked like you and me, but He possessed the essential nature of two things most of us do not have: the essential and unchanging characteristics of God (which we are largely *unable* to assume), and the essential and unchanging characteristics of a slave (which we are *unwilling* to assume).

> *He truly became man, not merely in outward appearance, but in thought and feeling. He who was the full image of God became the full image of Man. But even in this passage, where ὁμοίωμα so obviously means 'form,' there is still in the background the idea of the 'image' which is not identical with the original (the form of men) but like it...The divine figure entered history...*
>
> *The words ἑαύτον ἐκένωσεν (He emptied Himself) could suggest that He retained nothing of His divine nature. But the fact that as a man He accomplished what no other man could do—perfect obedience, leads to the conclusion that even as man He remained at the core of His being what He had been before."*
>
> *—J. Schneider*
> Theological Dictionary
> of the New Testament
> *Vol. V, p. 197*

Used only six times in the New Testament, ὁμοίωμα carries within it the possibility that Christ was more than human. He became a likeness of man with the true nature of God and the essence of a servant. It is for this reason that Jesus was able to tell His disciples, "If you have seen me, you have seen the Father."

THE APPEARANCE OF MAN

"...And being found in appearance *as a man..."*

> *σχῆμα (schema: form, appearance): everything which strikes the senses, the figure, bearing, discourse, actions, manner of life, outward representation, outward form, gestures, dress, etc.*

Every engineer and technician knows what a schematic is. Recently, when asked, one gave this definition:

> *A schematic shows, in abstract symbols, all of the essential characteristics of the function of the object, while showing none of the real form of the object. If one understands the symbols, he can tell just by observing the chart, the essential nature of the object.*

It does not merely indicate the coming of Jesus or His physical constitution, or the natural determination of His earthly life, or the shape of His moral character. It denotes the "mode of manifestation"—*how* He came; the form which was mere appearance rather than reality. This word always carries the factor of "outward decency in human conduct." The only other incidence in the New Testament of this word is in 1 Corinthians 7:31. This includes abstractions like dress, body language, expression—things which, when properly read, indicate the real person underneath. Those disciples, yearning to see and being attracted by the spiritual Jesus, could properly read the outward signs to see beyond to the essential God/Man. Those who saw but were blind, who heard but were deaf, only perceived the schematic.

So, by choosing these three words, Paul portrays our Christ as God, Servant, and the Perfect Man. He did not take the morphe of man, but the image, the homoioma, and the schema—the appearance and the lifestyle. His true nature was at once God and Servant. His sacrifice, then, while including His humiliating death on the Cross, also embraced His giving up all that was rightfully His because of His deity—even all that was rightfully His by being born as a man.

The result of this...

SUPREME EXALTATION

> *Therefore also God highly exalted Him, and bestowed on Him the name which is above every name, that at the name of Jesus every knee should bow, of those who are in heaven, and on earth and under the earth, and that every tongue should confess that Jesus Christ is Lord, to the glory of God the Father.*
>
> *—Philippians 2:9-11*

In conclusion, a bit more about this passage. Because of the relative rarity of the words we have studied, and comparing them with those in Paul's other writings, some analysts of the Philippian letter have suggested that possibly this passage—verses 5-11—may not have been written by Paul; that, much as a preacher today might insert a poem or the words of a song into his lesson, they suggest that perhaps the Apostle simply inserted the words of this hymn into this portion of his letter. This could very well be. When read in the Greek (even with our meager knowledge of their pronunciation), the passage exhibits both rhyme and meter. The first three verses begin with God exalting Jesus, then giving Him a holy name, then with tribute to the Christ from every knee and from every tongue, resulting in consummate glory to the Father—the Supreme Height.

From the status of slave, Jesus was exalted. His teaching, His actions, His intimate moments, and His moments before thousands, if not then, certainly now bear the Royal Stamp.

> *Come to Me, all who are weary and heavy-laden, and I will give you rest. Take My yoke upon you, and learn from Me, for I am gentle and humble in heart; and YOU SHALL FIND REST FOR YOUR SOULS. For My yoke is easy, and My load is light.*
>
> *—Matthew 11:28-30*

This is not a timid cowering Carpenter. He speaks these words and all of the others with the authority of a king possessing the undebatable mark of complete and universal dominion.

The Mind of Christ merits more study and emulation on the part of all of us. It leads us to believe that we have no rights, as we think of rights, and that God Himself will exalt us in due season.

The Mind of Christ—as shown by the 9th through 11th verses, also has a triumphant side as well as an humble one. We need to cultivate this as well. A good self-image because we are His is completely compatible with scripture. An image of joy, of faith in our abilities, of optimism, of love for the brethren—all because Jesus has been exalted to the right hand of God—these also are unity builders.

Let us strive with all our beings to cultivate within our souls...the Mind of Christ.

Study Questions

(1) Compare the text of this lesson with 2 Corinthians 8:9. In your own words, what is the essential meaning of these passages?

(2) In the last two lessons, we have studied some causes and cures for unity. How does this passage fit into that theme?

(3) There are at least three aspects to Jesus' great sacrifice which are mentioned in Philippians 2:6-8, one in each verse. Can you find them?

(4) What does "having the mind of Christ" mean in the light of the actions of Jesus described in Philippians 2:6-8?

(5) What does Paul mean in Philippians 2:10 when he says that "every knee should bow...*under* the earth"?

(6) Having partaken of Jesus' death in baptism, can we also emulate His victory as well as His humility?

(7) Is there a difference in Jesus being Christ and in His being Lord?

VI

Children of God, Without Blemish

Paul Addresses a Timeless and Universal Dilemma—That of Complaining

Text..............Philippians 2:14-16.

Memory Verse.....Philippians 2:14.

In the second chapter of Philippians, Paul has bared his soul to his beloved brethren concerning their unity. In the opening verses, he pleads with them to nurture every resource of loving compassion in order to lavish intimate fellowship among themselves.

He then draws upon the greatest example of all—that of the Master Giver—to show the degree to which love extends itself. He follows with an injunction to allow salvation to have its working, energizing way in our lives, because it is actually God who is at work within us. But in order for God to have His way in our lives, we must not block the positive, which radiates from Him.

OUR TEXT

> *Do all things without grumbling or disputing; that you may prove yourselves to be blameless and innocent, children of God above reproach in the midst of a crooked and perverse generation, among whom you appear as lights in the world, holding fast the word of life, so that in the day of Christ I may have cause to glory because I did not run in vain nor toil in vain.*
>
> *—Philippians 2:14-16*

GRUMBLING: SIGNPOST OF HUMANITY

Having reminded the Philippians that God is their energizer and their motivating force, Paul is now exhorting them as to the real purpose for which they are being energized:

> *Do all things without grumbling or disputing.*

> *"Murmurings" (goggusomos)...describes the low, threatening, discontented muttering of a mob who distrust their leaders and are on the verge of an uprising.*
>
> *—Barclay, p. 43*

Most comments on this verse seem to presume that "all things" means the work in the Lord's vineyard; but Paul himself does not limit these words to that interpretation; why should we? Indeed, if our religion is to be a way of life rather than being limited to a way of communal worship, how could we possibly consider that grumbling and complaining are acceptable also in realms other than the sacred?

We human beings have three main arenas in which we both exult and excel at grumbling and complaining. In no particular order of importance, they are:

(1) Against God;
(2) Against our fellow man; and
(3) Against ourselves.

When we complain against ourselves, it is often the result of poor self-image or low self-esteem. We are too fat, too short, too dumb, too shy, or too ______________ (fill in the blank et cetera infinitum ad nauseum). If we remember to acknowledge that it is, in fact, God who made us, our grumblings then become directed to Him. If we fail to remember this, then we fail to look to the only source of the solution to our problems. Should we choose to continue to grumble, we do indeed paint ourselves into a very bleak corner.

Even if an unpleasant situation is a result of our own doing, our grumblings often turn against God. Certainly they can encompass a God-given task, also.

> *They were to do all things without murmuring and arguing...because such expressions would obscure any thought of privilege in the inconveniences and hardships they were called upon to endure for Christ's sake. No one murmurs at a privilege. Complaining Christians have never caught the vision of the cross.*
>
> *—Herring, p. 72f*

And to quote Robertson:

> *These inward murmurings against God's will would easily turn to grumbling towards each other. People do not easily stop with resentment against God, but wish to blame somebody.*
>
> *—Robertson, p. 149*

Thus, grumblings against our fellow man can only jeopardize peace and unity. If we grumble against fellow workers on the job, the efficient, effective execution of that business is hampered; in the church, our souls as well as those of others are endangered.

These grumblings or murmurings begin as discontent, grow into resentment, and swell into rebellion. This is the silent, seething phase of the second word, without which we are to do "all things"—*disputing* (Greek, *dialogismos*: doubtings, questionings, arguments, contentions). If the first was inward, the second is a vocal, unpleasant manifestation of the first.

GRUMBLING: THE GREAT ROBBER

We like to grumble and complain! Children do this when they are bored or need attention. It always makes us feel superior to play the role of the critic, or perhaps to be the martyr—our situation, so terribly unpleasant and marginally bearable, of course having been caused completely by forces outside our own control. The teenager, to the total dismay and frustration of his parents, will grumble and complain against everything under the sun. These are the subconscious stirrings of rebellion with an eye toward independence; to be joyfully accepting (hence desirably congenial, of course) would mean never being able to leave the nest.

Pity the grumbler, but not because of the immediate target of his murmurings. He believes himself to be lashing out against his assailants in defense. In reality, the only one truly being harmed is the grumbler himself. This attitude is one of Satan's more potent weapons against the Christians—a robber of the most virulent stamp.

(1) Grumbling robs us of our *credibility*. Whether in the realm of work, recreation, or worship, the grumbler is faced with the likelihood that if he tries to sway men's minds in any direction, they will respond, "If he has everything so 'all together,' why does he complain so much?" His influence and his potential outreach are both significantly corroded by a complaining spirit. Conversely, the one who functions well without grumbling becomes the one sought after.

(2) Grumbling robs us of the *Christian growth* we so desperately need. Those ministering, building up, teaching, exhorting, serving, and planning have neither part nor lot with grumbling. The grumbler, constantly blaming others for his problems, never seems to get around to solving them (if they are real) or dissolving them (if they are imaginary), and so is inhibited in the business of getting on with living and growing. If he does manage to minister in a positive way, he is still hampered by the "I ought" instead of the "I may," and is usually hampered by an inordinate desire for recognition.

(3) Grumbling robs us of our *rewards and blessings* from God. This negative attitude is manifested in our efforts to exalt ourselves—with this, we have our own reward. If we have a grumbling spirit, it is likewise impossible simultaneously to have a spirit of thanksgiving.

> *Be anxious for nothing, but in everything by prayer and supplication with thanksgiving let your requests be made known to God. And the peace of God, which surpasses all comprehension, shall guard your hearts and your minds in Christ Jesus.*
>
> *—Philippians 4:6,7*

How can we have God's peace if we do not pray with thanksgiving? How can we "rejoice in the Lord always" (Philippians 4:4) if we are complaining? How can God reach us with His "happy messages" of warmth if we insulate our souls with the chilling cloak of complaint?

(4) Grumbling robs us of *"now" time*—the blessing of a scripture read, the touch of a child, the little cameos of God's surrounding natural beauty, the change of seasons, the preciousness of beautiful moments with loved ones, the laughter shared between the generations, a heartfelt prayer offered within a loving fellowship for one in need—all of these things and a thousand more God has infused into our walk with Him. They are our heritage, both as His earthly children and as His spiritual children. They are refuges for our souls, providing for us small but effective islands of peace among the strains and stresses of living. All are blocked, if not obliterated completely, by grumbling.

(5) Grumbling robs us first of our *ministry*, and then of our *potential to be helped.* It takes time and energy to grumble, and usually the grumbler has no motivation to encourage, lift up, comfort (see Chapter IV), and otherwise minister to those needing encouragement. He is the selfish one, a bottomless well of self-pity—always receiving, but never becoming filled. He is a drain on the emotional resources of those about him—a "black hole," if you will, within the Lord's body.

CHARACTERISTICS OF SALVATION

Away with murmuring and arguing! If we can manage to rid ourselves of these soul-blocks...

(1) We can be *doers.* Paul says to *do* all things without grumbling, etc. The "doing" itself is a great uplifter. A very successful minister once was asked how he managed to prevent strife and schism in his congregation. He looked very surprised and quickly replied, "Well, that's easy. The elders

and I keep 'em so busy they don't have *time* to fuss." The doers of this world are the only ones who are successful. Success fosters a healthy self-image; one with self-respect has no need to put others down, but can build them up. The doers possess vision, optimism, and zeal; they are the ones who see a job which needs to be done and say, "Okay, let's do it." Wise doers consider valid pros and cons but seldom, if ever, entertain grumbling and complaining.

(2) We can be *blameless*. Barclay says that this word, αμεμπτοσ (amemptos), expresses what the Christian is to the world.

> *His life is of such purity that none can find anything in it with which to find fault...He must not only be pure, but the purity of his life must be seen by all.*
>
> *—Barclay, p. 43*

(3) We can be *harmless* (ακεραιοσ [akeraios]; literally, "unmixed"; hence, without mixture of vice or deceit; sincere, innocent).

> *These Philippian Christians were to be outwardly and inwardly correct; that they might be no hindrance nor scandal to the name of Jesus Christ; and inwardly correct because no mere outward correctness can long be maintained without inward correctness.*
>
> *—J. W. Shepherd, p. 188*

(4) We can be seen as *children of God without blemish* in the midst of a crooked and perverse generation. "Without blemish" (αμομοσ [amomos]) is also translated "faultless" or "blameless," and is used in the sense of the perfect moral and religious piety to which Christians are obligated by virtue of their membership in the "called out" of these last days. It carries with it the idea of faultlessness before the judgment seat of God and Christ. So Paul is implying that we can be judged as "faultless" in the middle of a warped and perverted culture.

(5) We can be seen as *luminaries*—not as the light source itself, but as the moon or the stars which are made visible only in darkness. Darkness in the New Testament has always been so directly correlated with evil that often the two terms are used interchangeably. The word used here (a derivative of "phaino"—I shine) generally represents a reflected light or a light powered from some source—a lamp must burn oil or electricity; a candle, wax. The moon illuminates because of reflected light. The light source itself (used to describe Jesus in John 1:4) is "phos." This is the Light of Men because He *is* light. We are to be radiating His reflected light.

(6) We can be seen as *holding forth the word of life* to a very dark and sightless world. Speaking of the unrighteous, Peter wrote:

> *Then the Lord knows how...to keep the unrighteous under punishment for the day of judgment, and especially those who indulge the flesh in its corrupt desires and despise authority. Daring, self-willed, they do not tremble when they revile angelic majesties...But these, like unreasoning animals, born as creatures of instinct to be captured and killed, reviling where they have no knowledge, will in the destruction of those creatures also be destroyed, suffering wrong as the wages of doing wrong. They count it a pleasure to revel in the daytime. They are stains and blemishes, reveling in their deceptions, as they carouse with you: having eyes full of adultery and that never cease from sin; enticing unstable souls, having a heart trained in greed, accursed children...These are springs without water, and mists driven by a storm, for whom the black darkness has been reserved.*
>
> *—2 Peter 2:9,10, 12-14, 17*

These are the unrighteous for whom the Philippians and, in like manner, we today, stand as lights illuminating darkness.

Paul wanted to boast of the Philippians, and presumably they strove to be worthy of his pride. In this sense, boasting in the Lord is good—when we have labored in God's work with His strength and have brought forth His fruit, we can feel truly happy in this. Likewise, when we try to shine for those we love—parents, friends, mentors, those younger or weaker—we can take pride in a noble goal attained with the Lord's strength.

By accepting and imitating the self-sacrificing example of Christ, by allowing God to energize and empower us, and by casting grumbling and complaining from our makeup, we can be this kind of example to a lost and dying world.

Study Questions

(1) Name some of the "all things" that might apply in Philippians 2:14.

(2) Name the thing that is most disconcerting to you:
   (a) About yourself...Is it valid? Can you do something about it? If so, will you?
   (b) About your fellow man...Just might this be something of which you are guilty? (See Romans 2:1.)

(3) Other than the blessings mentioned in the text, what other things does grumbling rob us of?

(4) How would grumbling or questioning keep us from exhibiting the characteristics of salvation mentioned in Philippians 2:15,16?

(5) Transfer the adjectives "blameless," "harmless," "children of God without blemish," "luminary," and "holding forth the word of life" to your own situation. What can you do this week to manifest these more completely?

(6) Can you see any similarity in the unrighteous which Peter pictures in 2 Peter 2:9ff and the unrighteous of today? Any differences? What is your attitude toward these?

(7) Think of those persons in your life whom you see as being blameless and innocent; have you ever heard them complain? Conversely, think of one who never complains; do you think of him/her as pure or innocent?

VII

The Greatest Joy, The Greatest Sorrow

The Most Intense Feelings We Experience Come from the Trials and Triumphs of Those We Love Most Dearly

Text. . . . . Philippians 2:19-30.

Supplementary. . . . . Philippians 4:1,18.

Memory Verse. . . . . Philippians 2:29,30.

Paul's love for the Philippians is evidenced in every section of this comparatively brief letter. He agonized with them over their problems—largely the threat of disunity—and he rejoiced with them through their triumphs—their love for and faith in Christ and their steadfastness (Philippians 2:14-16). Indeed, the apostle's great heart was made both joyful and anguished—not by external circumstances, nor by his treatment at the hands of enemies of the cross, but by the triumphs and failures of those of his Christian family.

TIMOTHY: WILLING TO PLAY SECOND FIDDLE

But I hope in the Lord Jesus to send Timothy to you shortly, so that I also may be encouraged when I learn of your condition. For I have no one else of kindred spirit who will genuinely be concerned for your welfare. For they all seek after their own interests, not those of Christ Jesus. But you know of his proven worth that he served with me in the furtherance of the gospel like a

> *child serving his father. Therefore I hope to send him immediately, as soon as I see how things go with me; and I trust in the Lord that I myself also shall be coming shortly.*
>
> *—Philippians 2:19-24*

At the very first of this section, Paul tells the Philippians that he is sending Timothy to them for the purpose that Paul might also be cheered by news of them. This word for "cheered" is *eupsucho* and is very rare, found nowhere else in the New Testament. It speaks of "having courage," and was found in grave inscriptions as a final wish for the departed. His choice of this word might suggest that this would be their final exchange of communication. Because of his concern over their peace and harmony, this "news" might be to hear that they were working together as a unit. He also wanted to cheer them with the information that he was still well, and had joyfully received the gift that they had sent.

How Paul loved Timothy! In the second verse of each of the letters to Timothy, Paul calls him, respectively, "beloved child" and "true child in the faith." In Philippians 2:22, he speaks of Timothy's relationship with him as that "of a child serving with a father in the furtherance of the Gospel."

Paul's first recorded contact with Timothy is found in Acts 16:1. Timothy was the child of a Greek father and a Jewish mother, and Paul says in 2 Timothy 1:5 that Timothy had a sincere faith "...which first dwelled in your grandmother Lois and your mother Eunice." He was well-spoken of by the brethren in Lystra and Iconium. Apparently, this reputation was both genuine and widespread—the former because Paul wanted to take Timothy with them for the remainder of his second missionary journey, and the latter because all the Jews knew him.

We do not know how much time elapsed from the time that Paul met Timothy and it became apparent that he desired him to accompany them on that journey. But the duration seemed to be comparatively short.

Have you ever known someone just a short time but, because of their genuineness, their openness, and their acceptance of you, you felt as if you had been friends a lifetime and could be friends forever? Of course, you did not know all their shortcomings yet; but, because of the testimony of other Christians and their stature in the local congregation, you felt that even the more hidden aspects of their lives and personalities must ring true, that they are what they say they are and, anyway, you can accept them because they are accepting you in this manner. You can see Christ in each other! You can meet someone, know them a week, go to lunch once, and say "I've known you a lifetime" and mean it.

Paul sensed the sincere faith which dwelled in Timothy's heart, and he must have reasoned, "This is a good man to have working for God. I want him on my team." As Timothy was uncircumcised, this might indicate that he had been reared as a Greek. If so, Paul might have seen genuine potential in his ability to relate to the Greeks, whereas he (Paul) might not have been so readily accepted, being a Jew.

At any rate, Timothy did accompany Paul, and was present at the establishment of the church in Philippi. Paul says in Philippians 2:20 that there simply is no one else "who will genuinely be concerned for your welfare." Timothy loved that congregation as Paul did. He delighted in their progress and well-being. He was more like-minded—literally "equal-souled"—than any of Paul's other associates in Rome, who were busy going about their own affairs. The Philippians knew his worth (Philippians 2:22), as he had been present at their instigation and had visited them at least one other time (Acts 20:3-6). The word "worth" comes from a word which means "the testing which has shown character."

The result of all of this was that, eager to be about his Father's work, Timothy was willing to go to them.

EPAPHRODITUS: WILLING TO BE SPENT FOR THE LOCAL CONGREGATION

> *But I thought it necessary to send to you Epaphroditus, my brother and fellow-worker and fellow-soldier, who is also your messenger and minister to my need; because he was longing for you all and was distressed because you had heard that he was sick. For indeed he was sick to the point of death, but God had mercy on him, and not on him only but also on me, lest I should have sorrow upon sorrow. Therefore I have sent him all the more eagerly in order that when you see him again you may rejoice and I may be less concerned*

> *about you. Therefore receive him in the Lord with all joy, and hold men like him in high regard; because he came close to death for the work of Christ, risking his life to complete what was deficient in your service to me.*
>
> *—Philippians 2:25-30*

While Timothy was Paul's messenger to the Philippians, Epaphroditus was their messenger to him. While Timothy figured prominently in the establishment of other churches, in the actual writing of other of Paul's letters, and in many other references to varied activities, Epaphroditus is mentioned only in this letter (again in Philippians 4:18).

> *His is a good common, pagan name—one formed from the name of the Greek goddess Aphrodite.*
>
> *—Harrell, p. 107*

So, although he was not prominent in the New Testament church at large, take a second look at what he meant to Paul and the Philippian church. He was, to Paul, brother, fellow worker, and fellow soldier. Under Paul's tutelage, he ministered to the Philippian church. To them, he was their apostle and minister. He is the prototype of the one who would work continuously and self-sacrificially for the local church—ministering, caring, sacrificing, forbearing, eager to spend and be spent in whatever capacity needed—that individuals together and collectively might grow to be whole and one in Christ.

The Philippians loved Paul and wished to send him a gift to support him, both financially and emotionally, while in prison. They sent that gift with Epaphroditus. It is possible to extrapolate from Philippians 2:30 that he became ill on the journey, and risked his life to complete that service instead of stopping along the way to receive medical attention. At any rate, the Philippians had heard he was sick and were worried about him, which only compounded Epaphroditus' problem—he was worried over their concern for him!

INTERDEPENDENCE

What an inspiring message for us!

(1) We see the love the Philippians had for Paul, to send him such a beautiful gift.

(2) We see the love Epaphroditus manifested to the Philippians that he should be so desirous of seeing them, and so anxious about relieving their concern.

(3) We see the love of Epaphroditus for Paul and to the Philippians, in that he risked his life to complete the trust of his home congregation to bring the gift to Paul.

(4) We see the love between Paul and Epaphroditus. If he had died, Paul would have "sorrow upon sorrow." Indeed, God had shown mercy on Epaphroditus and had healed him—not only for his sake, but also that of Paul, as Paul could not have been able to bear another such heavy burden at this time.

How could the church in Philippi fail with these three great men nurturing, praying, and ministering to and for them? The love and cooperation felt between all parties makes itself felt in these few verses.

THE BARE BONES OF COMMITMENT

The "sorrow upon sorrow" that Paul would have felt had Epaphroditus died is the phrase from which the title of this lesson was drawn. The greatest sorrows in life come not from the loss of material possessions or status, but from the loss or separation of loved ones. Even if our separation comes from rebellion, emotional ostracism, lack of communication, misunderstanding, scandal, or whatever, still the greatest sorrows in any of our lives are caused by the people with whom we are most involved.

Likewise, the greatest joys also bless us through the people with whom we are most involved. Couples opt to have children—not because they are unaware that problems will occur, but because they know that involvement with other human beings produces the deepest satisfactions available to us. These rewards make the frustrations worthwhile.

Involving oneself in the life of another is always risky business. In Philippians 4:1, Paul again expresses the bittersweetness of his relationship to them.

> *Therefore, my beloved brethren (the exquisite sweetness), whom I long to see (the bitterness), my joy and crown (the satisfaction which comes from a fruitful relationship), so stand firm in the Lord (yearning for the very best for them), my beloved.*

To allow oneself voluntarily to be exposed to the hurts as well as the joys of a relationship is to allow oneself to be one step closer to what Jesus was. One of our weaknesses in the church today is that we tend to isolate ourselves from our brothers' and sisters' failures and shortcomings by not involving ourselves with them. Perhaps we are afraid they will "drain" us of our time, our emotional energy, or even of our financial resources. Perhaps they will.

Another point—that of the mobility of our society. A new family moves into the community, aligns themselves with the church, and works, loves, rejoices, cries, and labors with us. We grow to love, cherish, depend on, and support them. They enrich our lives. Then they leave! The inevitable pain results, and we are tempted to say, "Never again will I become so involved with people." The tendency is to begin to keep them "at arm's length."

What did we do to Christ, however? We drained Him of every last reserve; so much so that, within the sacrifice He made, even God Himself turned His back on our Lord.

How Jesus must grieve when one of us hurts Him, and how He must rejoice with us in moments of triumph, as our triumphs become His! When we rejoice with those who rejoice and weep with those who weep, are we not taking on part of their burden, perhaps risking being hurt, let down, or forsaken? Yes, just as Jesus did.

Is not this a command? Yes!

A WORD ABOUT FRIENDSHIP

The backbone of any relationship—brother/sister, husband/wife, even parent/child—is friendship. An excellent book currently available is *The Friendship Factor* by Alan Loy McGinnis. It is beyond the scope of this chapter to delve into all of the nooks and crannies of friendship which he explores, but the journey is well worth the time and money to hear him out. The overwhelming conclusion is that friendships are important—more important than most of us care to admit—and that a friend is truly a priceless treasure, irreplaceable, and well worth cultivating. If one has one or two cherished friendships in a lifetime, he is truly blessed.

This author took a mini-poll of acquaintances to determine what characteristics they deemed most valuable in a friend. Here are some of the answers:

A friend is someone...

...with whom you can be honest and open.

...with whom there is no need for a front, and who will still accept you for what you are.

...with whom you can share everything without fearing betrayal.

...who can inspire you to reach higher, deeper, and farther than you could ever reach on your own, and for whom you will do the same.

...with whom you share thoughts, emotions, feelings, ideas, dreams, confidences, possessions, and events.

...who has an understanding shoulder to cry on, who has a listening ear, and who understands your sadness and your laughter.

...with whom you can disagree, without anger.

...whom you can be around without needing to talk, or play games, or do some other specific activity—someone you can be quiet with.

...whom you love, and sex has nothing to do with it.

Friendship can be maintained with unconditional acceptance, unswerving loyalty, and mutual respect. It will be tarnished, if not shattered, by abandoning any of these.

From Kahlil Gibran:

> *And let your best be for your friend.*
>
> *If he must know the ebb of your tide, let him know its flood also. For what is your friend that you should seek him with hours to kill? Seek him always with hours to live. For it is his to feel your need, but not your emptiness.*

Because the greatest joy and the greatest sorrow lie in the interpersonal relationships which we choose to forge, our lives are enriched. The greatest sorrows make the greatest joys seem even more joyful, more fulfilling, and more abundant. The greatest joys fortify us for the sorrows, as the sorrows fortify us for greater worth in service.

Study Questions

(1) What do we know of Timothy's background; i.e., his family, home, etc.? (See Acts 16:1-3.) His role in primitive Christianity? (See Romans 16:21; 1 Corinthians 16:10,11; 2 Corinthians 1:1,19; 1 Thessalonians 3:2.)

(2) What was Paul's personal instruction to Timothy? (See 1 Timothy 4:6-16, 6:11-14.)

(3) Read 2 Timothy 3:10-15 to gain an understanding of shared mutual experiences. Read 2 Timothy 4:9-17 to learn of Paul's loneliness in prison and how he needed Timothy.

(4) What did Paul consider his relationship to Timothy to be? (1 Timothy 1:2; 2 Timothy 1:2; Philippians 2:22).

(5) What was Timothy's most important credential in relationship to the Philippian church? (Philippians 2:20).

(6) What do we know about Epaphroditus from other sources? What do we know about him through this letter?

(7) Find at least five other scriptures which deal with friendship. Try to include those describing friendship and those teaching how to maintain friendships. What do you consider to be the most important aspect of friendship? Share.

VIII

Things of Gain

Paul Lists Some Impressive Credentials of Which He Felt that He Could Be Proud

Text. . . . . Philippians 3:2-6.

Memory Verse. . . . . Matthew 6:33.

This lesson will be discussed in two parts, the second of which will be covered in the next lesson. In this, we will examine what Paul had been reared to think was important as a Jew, and will look at some things we possibly hold up as being of value to us.

Paul begins this section with a warning against the pernicious work of the Judaizing teachers—those who were teaching that after baptism, a man still needed to be circumcised to be acceptable to God. Then he states in Philippians 3:3:

> *For we are the true circumcision, who worship in the Spirit of God, and glory in Christ Jesus, and put no confidence in the flesh.*

These were the people who put confidence in worldly achievements, in human credentials, and in personal talents and abilities. Paul probably was expressly talking about circumcision and the Jews' reliance on this outward sign of a covenant with God; but he is also stressing the entire approach to any religion which emphasizes the outward, human achievement.

WHAT PAUL HAD ATTAINED AS A JEW

Circumcised on the eighth day—Not when he was 13, as he would have been as a descendant of Ishmael, or when he was an adult, as a

Jewish proselyte might have been, but on the eighth day. He was ritually pure.

Of the nation of Israel—Regularly descended of Jacob; not from proselytes, but by race; one of God's chosen people.

Of the tribe of Benjamin—From Jacob's favorite wife, a tribe which gave Israel its first king, which remained loyal to Jehovah when Jeroboam revolted; which remained loyal to the worship of Jehovah, and which contained within its boundaries the Holy City and the Temple.

A Hebrew of Hebrews—Paul was originally from Tarsus, a city in Asia Minor; so, although he was not born in the land of Palestine, his parents spoke Hebrew and practiced Hebrew cultural ritual in their home.

So, in the first part of Philippians 3:5, Paul describes his Jewish inheritance—his by accident of birth—with ritual purity, racial purity, and cultural purity. Now he describes his Jewishness in terms of his own activity.

As to the Law, a Pharisee—A sect which arose during the inter-biblical period for the purpose of retaining Jewish orthodoxy in the face of the spread of Greco-Roman culture. It was created to maintain the purity of Jehovah worship and the practice of Mosaical Law; marked by strictness and conservatism.

As to zeal, a persecutor of the Church—Greek participle: *deokon*: to put in rapid motion; to pursue; to follow eagerly; to persecute. We all remember with what intensity, zeal, and abandon he carried out this persecution.

As to righteousness which is in law, blameless—Because all men have sinned (Romans 3:23), Paul could not be counting himself here as sinless. He is evidently referring to his ritual emphasis—that he totally kept the ritual part of the law.

The things Paul counted as good and righteous were based on confidence in the flesh, both what was his because of his country and his race, and because of what he himself had achieved. It was totally a legalistic mindset. He drew his significance as a person from his Jewish framework. He was secure in these fleshly credentials of his.

Keeping in mind his Jewish heritage and these things that were of immense significance in his life, let us consider his conversion. There are three accounts in Acts of this—one by Luke and two from Paul's lips, as recorded by Luke.

While thus engaged as I was journeying to Damascus with the authority and commission of the chief priests, at midday, O King, I saw on the way a light from heaven, brighter than the sun, shining all around me and those who were journeying with me. And when we had all fallen to the ground, I heard a voice saying to me in the Hebrew dialect,

"Saul, Saul, why are you persecuting Me? It is hard for you to kick against the goads."

And I said, "Who art Thou, Lord?"

And the Lord said, "I am Jesus whom you are persecuting. But arise, and stand on your feet; for this purpose I have appeared to you, to appoint you a minister and a witness not only to the things which you have seen, but also to the things in which I will appear to you; delivering you from the Jewish people and from the Gentiles, to whom I am sending you.

—Acts 26:12-17

Notice the phrase in Acts 26:14, "It is hard for you to kick against the goads." Saul did say, "Who art Thou, Lord?" He knew that this vision and this voice were from God, but he had thought that he was serving God. So he found this dramatic effort to get his attention confusing.

It is evident from his later activities that the Apostle Paul had an unusual gift of sensitivity and perception. He could see the beauty of the lives of those in Christ. No doubt he knew the Christian story; he knew of events and of Christ's life. He had been witness to the incredibly moving sermon of Stephen. Jesus would never have said this to Paul had it not been true.

Saul, it is very painful to you to be treating beautiful Christians like this. You know the story; you can see the results in their lives. I AM JESUS OF NAZARETH WHOM YOU ARE PERSECUTING!

Why had Paul continued to persecute Christians? Jesus said that it hurt Paul to kick against the goads. Why did he continue? THOSE FLESHLY CREDENTIALS!

> *(I was) circumcised the eighth day, of the nation of Israel, of the tribe of Benjamin, a Hebrew of Hebrews; as to the Law, a Pharisee; as to zeal, a persecutor of the church; as to the righteousness which is in the Law, found blameless!*

> *I am a Jew. I am in a covenant with God through Abraham. I am righteous because I keep the Law completely. I feel badly about persecuting these people; they have a joy, a calmness, and a love that I don't have; but those feelings must be pushed aside: I AM A JEW!*

One present-day psychiatric source has suggested that possibly Paul's perception of the goodness inherent in Christianity began with the angelic decorum of Stephen at his death (Acts 6:15f) and continued to broaden to the point of the Damascus Road incident. Stephen also had given his audience, Saul included, an anger-inspiring, albeit truthful, dose of reality:

"You don't love; you hate."

Saul could perceive this as well. It is possible that his intellectual allegiance to Judaism and rejection of Christianity coupled with his attraction to the vitality of the Way were, therefore, creating such internal turmoil that his activity degenerated into a frenzied drive to eliminate the supposed source of the conflict—the Christians themselves. According to this source, then, Christ had to intervene in order to preserve the man against self-destruction. The incident shocked Saul into an hypnotic state from whence he could then be led into the desired behavior.

At any rate, Jesus had shattered his security framework. In effect, He said, "Paul, you are laboring under the false security of an outdated, superseded structure." All of the things in which Paul had placed his security were dissolved. His encounter with the Christ and subsequent three days of bleakness left him nothing whatever to stand on. In the next lesson, we will study "the REST of the story" but, for now, let us consider some of the things on which we might place our security.

THINGS OF GAIN

The credentials of Saul which were so important to him and other Jews WERE important. The following things in this discussion ARE important. Let us not minimize these in our lives. We simply need to take a fresh inventory. First, each should ask himself or herself: "I would lose my security, or I would feel very insecure, if I lost ______________" or "I would have no significance as a person if I did not have my ______________." Here are a few possible "blank-fillers" which have bothered some people.

(1) *Education.* Education IS important. It teaches one to think, challenging the mental processes, and can inspire one to greater goals with more confidence. It builds new and different perspectives. But if one crowns his formal education by placing his personal significance in the degree he has, he has missed the point of the education experience. Education is a humbling experience. One learns how much he does not know! More than just giving one the answers, education really just gives one a glimpse at the questions. Learning has been called an island in the ocean of ignorance. If the island gets bigger, so does the shoreline of ignorance. THE TRULY WISE MAN KNOWS HOW LITTLE HE KNOWS.

(2) *Job, Career, Vocation.* If I lost my job, what would happen to my worth as a human being? What happens to my personal sense of worth if someone else is awarded my long-awaited promotion? Any career for many reasons can come to a grinding halt.

(3) *Things.* If my house is robbed and I lose that beautiful new set of china so carefully accumulated, would I cease to be worthwhile as a person? Since acquiring that china, this writer has been more motivated to be a better and more frequent hostess, and cook with more elegance. But, if it were lost or destroyed, would that mean I should stop? We cannot place our significance in the kind of car we drive, the clothes we wear, our homes, or such like. These are not permanent. TRUE MATERIAL SECURITY LIES NOT IN THE THINGS ONE HAS, BUT IN THE THINGS ONE CAN DO WITHOUT.

(4) *Beauty, Good Looks.* How many individuals believe themselves to be worthwhile because they are physically attractive? How many believe that WHEN (not IF) they lose their attractiveness, they will cease being worthwhile? Think of the money spent—health clubs, cosmetics, cosmetic surgery, athletic equipment, diet plans, books, pills, special diet aids, hair coloring; the list is endless! Yes, we need to care for our bodies. Yes, we need to look as good as we can, and be as healthy as we can, for as long as we can. But, no—it really is not important enough to go into a froth if one's lipstick and nail polish do not match! When your looks fade, will you need a psychiatrist?

(5) *Health.* If we look at history, and at the third world nations today, we see illness, malnutrition, disease—hardship of all kinds. Good health is truly the exception rather than the norm. We should be humbly grateful for the good health that we enjoy, doing the best and most healthful things in our power to preserve it. We should be aware of it, and we should thank God for it. Too many of us, however, take our good health for granted; then, when illness overtakes us, we feel as though we alone have been singled out as the object of God's wrath. We all know people who talk only about their illnesses, non-stop. There is at least one elderly lady who will read nothing except *Prevention* magazine (she is afraid that her eyes will wear out) and articles on health, vitamins, and such like—and her conversation is limited to this field. Many Americans have made a religion out of health. It is important, but it should be kept in proper perspective.

(6) *Family.* Do I live through my family? Are my husband's/wife's successes my successes? They'd better be! Are my children's achievements my achievements? They'd better be! Are his/her interests my interests? YES! But does my significance lie in the fact that I am only my husband's wife (or vice versa)? Does my morale depend solely on his/her moods? If my spouse dies, will I become a non-person because my sole identity rested in him/her?

Children—do I live only through them? What if they leave home, reject my moral values, go into a life of crime, take up an occupation foreign to my interests, fail a grade in school, or (Heaven forbid!) drop a key pass in the last few seconds of a critical game? Am I going to fall victim to the "empty nest" syndrome because my identity was inextricably entwined in theirs? Children had *better* be important to us if we have them, but we had best not have our own personal importance dependent on them.

(7) *People.* Let us beware of putting too many of our emotional eggs into the people basket. Political leaders, preachers, elders, Bible school teachers, bosses, public school teachers—anyone in a leadership capacity, and having leadership responsibilities, possesses the capability of damaging the trust (if not the faith) of the people commensurate with his office. Especially regard the functions of leaders in the church—preachers, elders, and Bible school teachers. They are every bit as human as you are. Build the church around Christ, not the preachers. Put your security in Christ, not the elders. Do not depend on your Bible school teachers to be perfect. All of these people need your love, your comfort, your support, and your understanding when they fail (*especially* when they fail), but none of them needs your worship. If one's security rests on the stature of an elder or evangelist, and he betrays that trust, one's security will fail him. Mark those like Diotrephes who seem to seek your worship.

(8) *The Church.* Jesus loved the church and gave Himself for it (Ephesians 5:25). It is made up of those who are saved; when we are saved, we are added by God to its heavenly roll. But just because one's name is on a church roll somewhere does not mean that he/she is automatically "in." We are all just human beings. Not one of us can save another. Also, if a congregation is engaged in many wonderful works, that does not give any individual member a heavenly ticket. WE CANNOT GET TO HEAVEN ON THE COATTAILS OF OTHER CHRISTIANS. The church is the most wonderful body of human beings on God's green earth; but the church, because of her humanness, may let you down. Let us strive to help her to grow into the perfect bride of Christ; love, support, and exhort, but do not let church membership either be a substitute for your relationship with God or the seat of your personal security.

(9) *Your Ministry.* One of our Abilene preachers recently presented a talk on the subject of spiritual growth. One of the statements he made should become a powerful guideline for all Christians. He said that he finally came to realize that his pulpit ministry was standing between himself and his God. He saw that his goals were coming to be eloquence, profundity, trying to impress his elders and his congregation, devoting long hours toward improving his Bible class lessons, etc. It finally came to him that he was putting this ministry first in his life, and that his family was second, leaving his relationship with his God a shabby third.

Whether our ministry is one of prayer, busing, visiting, prisons, teaching, or whatever, we *should* give it everything we have. It *is* important.

But what is the most important thing in this life?

> *But seek first His kingdom and His righteousness; and all these things shall be added to you.*
>
> —*Matthew 6:33*

To which we might add:

> *For your heavenly Father knows that you need all these things.*
>
> —*Matthew 6:32*

Study Questions

(1) List in order five or more things which you think are important.

(2) What are some of the things that Paul, earlier in his life, thought were important?

(3) Why did he count these things as being so important to him?

(4) What are some activities which church members engage in which could be considered "law-keeping"? What makes the difference in their being "law-keeping" and genuine service?

IX

The Most Important Thing in Paul's Life

Paul Tells the Secret of His Motivation, the Driving Force of His Power, and the Wellspring of His Hope

Text. . . . . Philippians 3:7-11.

Supplementary. . . . . Philippians 3:20,21.

Memory Verse. . . . . Philippians 3:8.

NEW VALUES FOR OLD

> *Therefore if any man is in Christ, he is a new creature; the old things passed away; behold, new things have come.*
>
> *—2 Corinthians 5:17*

In the last lesson, we examined some factors in Paul's life on which he had built his life structure—the things which gave his actions significance, and his being personal security.

Then he met Christ on the Damascus Road.

> *But whatever things were gain to me, those things I have counted as loss for the sake of Christ. More than that, I count all things to be loss in view of the surpassing value of knowing Christ Jesus my Lord, for whom I have suffered the loss of all things, and count them but rubbish in order that I may gain Christ, and may be found in Him, not having a righteousness of my own*

> *derived from the Law, but that which is through faith in Christ, the righteousness which comes from God on the basis of faith, that I may know Him, and the power of His resurrection and the fellowship of His sufferings, being conformed to His death; in order that I may attain to the resurrection from the dead.*
>
> *—Philippians 3:7-11*

His life had been turned around. He had literally been saved from himself by the intervention of Christ. After three years of foundation-building in the Arabian desert (Galatians 1:15-18), his new identity firmly established in Christ, he became Christ's ambassador to the Gentiles.

Three times in Philippians 3:7-9, Paul mentioned the word "loss." Everything that he had counted as a plus in his life became as refuse; literally, "dung." In Philippians 3:8, the language indicates that, indeed, he also counted as loss *everything* that others counted as gain as well. He had compared the values which he had seen on earth, and they had all come up short in view of the "surpassing worth of knowing Christ," for the *sake* of Christ, and for the *gain* of Christ.

Remember Mary, who broke the alabaster flask to release the ointment to anoint Jesus? In terms of all of the wealth of all of the world throughout eternity, even that expensive-at-the-time gift seems insignificant. But look at the impact that has made on the hearts and lives of men! Unbeknownst to her, that event blessed her with a place in history. The "greatest giver in history"—the widow with her two mites—was given a place in history. They both gained immeasurably from sacrificial giving. There are some Christians who do not know what it is to give their all for Christ, and they are missing untold blessings.

> *No one who has laid down all things for Christ ever seems dissatisfied with the exchange. On the contrary, those who have done so seem possessed of a joy unknown to others...*
>
> *—Herring, p. 82*

In this passage, Paul presents Christ as the criterion by which *all* values are to be determined. He writes about five things primarily which he had gained in his new relationship in Christ:

(1) *A New Position.* Paul uses the phrase "in Christ" (or "in the Lord" or "in Him") 164 times. When he became a Christian, Paul was immediately cognizant of this new position of security, and proceeded with all of his life's activities and writings to portray its power and its glory.

His safety and ours lie in our position "in Christ," but our fruitfulness lies in the extent to which Christ is "in us" (John 15:5).

(2) *A New Righteousness.*

> *The great basic problem of life is to find fellowship with God and to be at peace and in friendship with Him. The way to that fellowship is through righteousness, through the kind of life and spirit and attitude to Himself which God desires. Because of that, righteousness nearly always for Paul has the meaning of "a right relationship with God."*
>
> *—Barclay, p. 62*

For so long, Paul had presumed that this relationship could be attained through the characteristics of Jewishness in which he had trusted. He had striven for righteousness in his privilege by birth, and through his own works through the Law. He could not reach a right relationship with God, however, except through Jesus Christ—a righteousness of power, strength, and completeness—a gift, freely given, when one is "in Christ."

(3) *A New Power.* The power of the Resurrection can mean many things to many people, but for Paul, it was not simply a day marked on God's celestial calendar. To Martha, Christ Himself had revealed, "*I* am the Resurrection." So for us, Barclay lists three different directions in which the Resurrection of Christ provides us with a great dynamic:

(a) It is the guarantee of the importance of this life and the body in which we live. Our bodies are the Temple of the Holy Spirit (1 Corinthians 6:19,20), and are the only vessels God has to do His work on earth.

(b) It is the guarantee that in life and in death and beyond death the presence of the Risen Lord is always with us; death is not the end of life.

(c) It is the guarantee that there is life to come (Romans 8:11; 1 Corinthians 15:14f).

(4) *A New Fellowship.* A part of Paul's gain was to come to know Christ more intimately through the fellowship of His sufferings. Paul counted suffering for Christ a privilege. Likewise, there is no fellowship so sweet as helping to bear the burden of the suffering friend. This author will shout personal good news from the rooftops, but it is only to a chosen few she will bare intimacies of personal suffering, temptation, and weakness. We feel free to share our sorrows and heartaches only with the closest of our friends.

> *Paul had come to know Christ in the sacred intimacy of His sufferings as he could have known Him in no other way.*
>
> *—Herring, p. 85*

(5) *A New Purpose.* We will consider this carefully in the next lesson.

PAUL'S PRIME MOVER

The knowledge of Christ, to Paul, was of surpassing worth; the word "surpassing" in the Greek means literally "having over;" a more elegant definition—to hold above, to stand out above; to overtop, to surpass, to excel—in other words, the knowledge of Christ and gaining Him HAD IT OVER any external ritual, cultural framework, or racial inheritance. To KNOW Christ, as Paul continues in Philippians 3:10, meant "to know the POWER of His resurrection; and that I might know the FELLOWSHIP of His sufferings."

The surpassing worth of the knowledge of Christ, to be found in Him, to be righteous before God, to know the continuing power portrayed because of His resurrection, and to have His fellowship—this was the Prime Mover, the alpha and the omega of Paul's life. And this must be the single most important element in each of our lives. Everything else, anything else, is secondary.

Again, recall Matthew 6:33, the memory verse in the last lesson.

A DIFFICULT PARADOX

To the new Christian, one of the immediate paradoxes of the New Testament makes itself felt in Christ's injunction:

> *If anyone wishes to come after Me, let him deny himself, and take up his cross, and follow Me. For whoever wishes to save his life shall lose it; and whoever loses his life for My sake and the gospel's shall save it.*
>
> *—Mark 8:34b,35*

This equivalent language is found in no fewer than five places in the Gospels. Most of us will follow Christ a certain distance; but when we ultimately come to realize that He demands *us*—not a portion of our income, a segment of our time, allegiance when convenient, or token service, but *all* of each one of us—we tend to balk.

"No, Lord; not *all* of me. I still want to keep my little pet, Vice; after all, whaddya expect?"

"All of you."

"But Lord, I've got my job and my family. I'm told to care for them, right? I mean, how can I go to church three times a week? I've gotta work for a living, you know."

"Christian, I want you—all of you. Take a leap of faith; embrace and *try* the promise that all of these things will be added to you. Either that, or you will find that they are no longer that important. How can I give you all of Me, if you will not give all of yourself?"

> *Ask, and it shall be given to you; seek, and you shall find; knock, and it shall be opened to you.*
>
> *—Matthew 7:7*

Paul has taken his stand; he has made his choice. The sublime excellency of knowing Christ (not the knowledge gained from hearsay or from objective observation, but that knowledge which comes from the most intimate personal experience) has overtopped any value or experience that he might have counted as worthwhile. To be at one with God through the righteousness attained through faith in Christ fulfills the ultimate longing of the human spirit.

Life is a mystery at best, full of change and surprises. Relative values change with the years. For Christ's sake, however, and for His permanence, Paul had discarded these old important values, and he had paid the price. But it was worth the price! The price is high but, once on the other side of payment, it is negligible. It will never be missed.

> *Again, the kingdom of heaven is like a merchant in search of fine pearls, who, on finding one pearl of great value, went and sold all that he had and bought it.*
>
> *—Matthew 13:45,46 (RSV)*

The exchange was worth everything he had! What does the New Testament tell us if not this one thing—*in every aspect of our lives, knowing Christ is the one facet to be desired above all else.*

Study Questions

(1) What was the most important factor in Paul's life?

(2) Give an example of what it means to you:
- (a) To gain Christ.
- (b) To be found in Him.
- (c) To know Christ.

(3) What have you lost which the world might have considered as gain?

(4) Give an example of righteousness based on Law, and one of righteousness based on faith.

(5) How can one attain a right relationship with God?

(6) How can we appropriate "the power of the resurrection" in our lives?

(7) The results of a right relationship with God are described in Philippians 3:10; make a list.

X

Forgetting What Lies Behind

Paul Discusses the Desirability of Pressing On to the Perfect Mark— the "Upward Call of God in Christ Jesus"— Even Though We Are Imperfect

Text. . . . . Philippians 3:12-16.

Memory Verse. . . . . Philippians 3:13,14.

We are all so imperfect, so fallible, so human! We can ill afford to be critics, for we ourselves are so encompassed with our own faults. In the preceding section, Paul has discussed what it means to know Christ; to Paul, it meant to share in His sufferings and to grow to be so much like Christ—in, through, and because of the power of the Resurrection—that he, Paul, would be perfect enough to be raised from the dead with Christ. It meant that Christ was everything to Paul, and knowing Him was worth the price.

However, in the first parts of Philippians 3:12,13, he states that he has not attained this stature commensurate with the goals of Philippians 3:11.

> *Not that I have already obtained it, or have already become perfect, but I press on in order that I may lay hold of that for which also I was laid hold of by Christ Jesus. Brethren, I do not regard myself as having laid hold of it yet; but one thing I do: forgetting what lies behind and reaching forward to what lies ahead, I press on toward the goal for the prize of the upward call of God in Christ Jesus. Let us therefore, as many as are perfect, have this attitude; and if in anything you have a*

different attitude, God will reveal that also to you; however, let us keep living by that same standard to which we have attained.

—Philippians 3:12-16

He begins this section with the commendable attitude of every good elder, deacon, preacher, teacher, parent, or any other Christian—"I haven't arrived; I haven't reached perfection yet. This readiness to live with Christ is something I have not yet attained." There is a very important lesson which Paul focuses on here, which is so very close to where we live. He has hinted to at least four great truths which modern psychology is just beginning to discover to be essential for us.

LET YOURSELF BE HUMAN

The first is that it is normal and "okay" to be human—truly, that no one has "arrived." Having to be perfect continually is really an awesome burden! A little egg on the face once in a while is very good for the complexion! When we begin to allow ourselves (and others too, please!) some weaknesses, to look at those weaknesses with honesty, and then to do something about them with the Lord's help (and perhaps with professional counselors), then we can begin to enjoy life. Ron Bryant's list of "Enemies of Inner Peace" is well worth "an inward journey" (see App. A).

In the preceding chapter, we named five new values which Paul had gained with his new relationship in Christ. We studied:

(1) A New Position.

(2) A New Righteousness.

(3) A New Power.

(4) A New Fellowship.

In this lesson, we want to discuss No. 5:

(5) *A New Purpose*. In Philippians 3:12, Paul had said, "Christ Jesus has made me His own." Another translation: "...has taken hold of me." Like Paul, Christ has now taken hold of *me*. I have had, and always will have, the universal choice to

sin—I have the choice to drink, or be promiscuous, or beat down my fellow workers to get ahead, or to do any number of things, because God has given each of us that choice. If I or any other Christian willfully continues the pursuit of sin, however, he or I will lose the option of forgiveness (Hebrews 10:26).

However, when tempted, each should ask himself, "To whom do I belong? Whose am I? Who struggled into this bleak wilderness of sin to bring me back? Who *has taken hold of me*?"

> *What man among you, if he has a hundred sheep and has lost one of them, does not leave the ninety-nine in the open pasture, and go after the one which is lost, until he finds it? And when he has found it, he lays it on his shoulders, rejoicing. And when he comes home, he calls together his friends and his neighbors, saying to them, "Rejoice with me, for I have found my sheep which was lost!"*
>
> —*Luke 15:4-6*

I no longer belong to myself, but "Christ Jesus has taken hold of me, and made me His own." I have not, however, obtained that perfect Christian walk—I do not consider that I have made perfection my own. I still have human weaknesses, human values, human hurts and bruises.

So, in order to deal with this, in order to allow Christ's healing blood to cleanse, and grace to bestow its divine gift, I must accept myself with all my imperfections. There still remains the big gap between me and that perfect attainment mentioned in Philippians 3:11. Paul sensed this conflict. Reminding us that Christ still has made us his own, he presents to us his second and third great truths.

ONE THING I DO

This holds great value for those who must work under tension. If one can discern what the single most important task is, and then apply himself to that one task, a load will be lifted—lifted more efficiently at that—and stress will be lessened. Do the task; when finished, address the lesser activities.

My husband starts studying for his Bible lesson, and the first thing I know, he will ask me to discuss first one Greek word, then another, which leads first to one idea, then another. I will finally ask, "What on earth is this lesson about, anyway?" We will be far afield, "chasing rabbits." A thorough treatment of the original lesson remains just beyond reach.

Many a Christian has allowed a sense of "thronging duties" to distract his attention from the one task at hand, and thus to subtract from the joy which doing that task should yield to him and to those whom he is trying to serve.

Now, Paul, what *is* that one thing you do?

FORGET THOSE THINGS IN THE PAST!

> *But one thing I do: forgetting what lies behind and reaching forward to what lies ahead, I press on toward the goal for the prize of the upward call of God in Christ Jesus.*
>
> —*Philippians 3:13b-14*

This is Paul's third great psychological principle. Let us look at some things which drag us down and hold us back.

(1) *Forget past sins.* This guilt from the past is extremely burdensome. It weights down our self-image to the point that at times we cannot even find it! God has, through Christ, forgiven us when we take Christ on in baptism, when Christ makes us His own. Can we not forgive ourselves then? Easy to say; hard to do! Accept His promise by faith that He remembers these things not at all.

(2) *Forgive, forgive, forgive!* If you are young, forgive your parents. Accept their humanness as you accept your own. They made mistakes in rearing you. Most of them made some horrendous mistakes, but you are accountable now.

You are responsible for your own life. You can search out the help and support you need to work it out. You can rely on the cleansing meditations of prayer and study in God's word. The Lord will use your new insight for His glory. Try to cast these old hurts aside. Nothing is so permanent that you, love, and the Lord cannot heal it.

If you are middle-aged, forgive yourself. You have done some stupid things, made some foolish remarks, thought some hideous thoughts, and felt some unspeakable emotions. Admit it to God and to yourself. Look it straight in the eye and call it "Yesterday"! If you need to make something right between you and another person, shore up your courage by reading Matthew 5:23,24 and Matthew 18:15f, go to that person with prayer, and make that right. Then *forget* those things which are behind.

If you are old, forgive your children. Forget their faults, which may even be behind them now. Most people are trying to grow better. Help them; support them; acknowledge their struggles, and recognize their growth. If they were obstinate, rebellious, critical, and disrespectful in their youth, look for and expect improvement. People (usually children, but also often adults) will act the way you expect them to.

(3) *Allow neither the past nor the future to dominate the present.* "Forgetting" is a process. Paul's use of this word reflects the Jewish concept of "remembering." To "remember" something was to lift it out of the dead past and thereby to make it a dynamic force in the present. Doing this can completely over-burden your present. These situations often are described by statements that begin by saying, "If only..."

Also, discard the *burden* of the future. *Planning* and *burden* are two different concepts. *Planning* implies constructive and aggressive action, the self-discipline of preparation and organization, the mindset of being good to yourself so you need not become hopelessly mired in a predicament which could have been avoided with pre-planning. But the *burden* of the future is almost always described by statements which begin with, "What if..." A line from Sir William Osler brings the point:

> *The load of tomorrow added to that of yesterday, carried today, makes the strongest falter.*

(4) *Refuse to cling to your past securities.* Once you had security and significance in your job, your family, your preacher (discussed two chapters ago); but now, your security is in Christ. Forget those things which are behind.

(5) *Forget present slights and pettiness.* "She didn't speak to me yesterday." "She didn't notice my new dress." "My husband didn't compliment dinner tonight." "The boss doesn't realize what a good man I really am." Let Jesus be so strong in you as to be impervious to these slights. If Sister Fistermeister snubbed you, that is her problem, not yours. If your husband does not brag on your dinner (first, make sure that it is worth bragging on!), that is *his* problem, not yours. If the boss does not recognize your abilities, adopt Ephesians 6:5-8 and Colossians 3:22,23 as part of your soul, and then follow it; it should not take him long.

Yes—we do need affirmation from others, and it is nice to have. But if you do not get it as regularly as you like, do not let that bog you down. LET YOUR FAITH IN CHRIST, YOUR SECURITY IN HIM, AND HIS STRENGTH IN YOU MAKE YOU BIGGER THAN THESE SLIGHTS. Let your faith lift you above them. Because of His faith in the Father, Christ was able to handle far greater injustices.

(6) *Forget the "slave" mentality.* The slave says, "How much do I *have* to give?" "How often do I *have* to go to church?" "Do I *have* to visit?" The slave does only what he *has* to do to save his neck. There is no place for this mindset in the Lord's vineyard.

Paul's fourth great truth...

I PRESS ON TO THE GOAL

He is saying, "I am stretching, straining, or struggling now to attain this high calling, this marvelous perfection in Christ Jesus." And he says that he is "pressing on." Do you remember the little word "deokon" which Paul used when he was telling of persecuting the church? We reviewed the zeal and abandon with which he pursued this goal. His word here for "pressing on" is the same word that he is using to describe this quest.

> *I follow after; I pursue; I persecute; with the same energy, the same zeal, enthusiasm, and determination, with which I persecuted the church.*

"I press on..." To what, Paul? "...for the *prize*; for the *reward*; for the *surpassing worth* of the *knowledge* of Christ; for the *upward call in Christ Jesus!*"

Christian friends, this is the single most important element in our lives. Everything else—anything else—is secondary. Our relationship with God, in and through Jesus Christ, is the only thing in which we can place our security. IT IS LITERALLY MORE SECURE THAN BREATHING, MORE VITAL THAN EATING. IT IS THE ONE AND ONLY THING WHICH CAN NEVER BE TAKEN FROM US.

Again, Christ said it best:

> *Seek first the kingdom of God, and His righteousness; and all these things shall be added to you.*
>
> *—Matthew 6:33*

> *As many as are perfect, have this attitude; and if in anything, you have a different attitude, God will reveal that also to you; however, let us keep living by that same standard to which we have attained.*
>
> *—Philippians 3:15,16*

PRIZES TO AIM FOR

Let us consider a few specific goals which will help us to reach this prize of the upward call—some suggestions for straining, stretching, and reaching upward to the things which lie before.

(1) Take the *whole* Bible. We have many wrong reasons for studying. Instead, let us plead, "Lord, let my knowledge of this passage draw me closer, make me Thine, and help me to

change into Christ's image." And then, proceed to make all of the Bible your own, even if it means changing pet ideas.

(2) *Claim God's promises.* He promises to bless us, take care of us, give us strength when we need it, forgive us, lead us, love us—the list goes on and on. Do you believe Him? Do you take Him at His word? Try His promises.

(3) *Live with power.* We *can* live with power if we quit trying to be good all by ourselves. We can live with power when we allow Christ's love, beauty, and goodness to shine through us. We can live with power when we quit trying to straddle the wishy-washy fence, and start depending on God's Word and God's Holy Spirit to live in and direct our lives. We can live with power if we long to be like Christ and the Father, earnestly seeking to grow into their images. Our faults and shortcomings do not have to be a permanent condition!

(4) *Let God bring us around to Himself.* Read Philippians 1:6, 2:12,13, and 3:9. We have to want to, but He has not left us alone without the means by which we can align our lives with His.

(5) Take the *whole* Gospel:

   (a) We need to know the *Law.*

   (b) We need *Grace*—continual cleansing as we walk in the light.

   (c) We need *Works*—in order to fulfill the perfect law of liberty and to spread the kingdom.

   (d) We need *Faith*—the core that shelters us from emotional storms, within and without.

   (e) We need *Love*—unselfish, Christlike, enabling us to accept our brothers and sisters with their weaknesses, and them to accept us with ours. Love is the quickening agent which brings the Law to life, gives meaning to works, makes faith very real and vital for us, and is the reason that grace can liberally be given and received.

   (f) We need to remember God's *Justice*—the sixth vital tenet of the Gospel. With all of the injustice there is in the world, what God of love would allow that ultimately to be left unpunished? God's justice is certain.

When we can totally incorporate into our lives a balanced Gospel—one which gives equal stress to Law, Grace, Works, and Justice, all bound together and quickened by Love—we can truly begin to emulate Paul's example which he mentions in Philippians 3:17:

> *Brethren, join in following my example, and observe those who walk according to the pattern you have in us.*

(6) *Taking the whole Gospel, embrace the "son" mentality* (Romans 8:14-16; Galatians 4:1-9). The son will do whatever he can to make the family prosper financially, emotionally, and spiritually. It is *his* inheritance; he has a stake in the growth and direction of the family.

(7) *Remember that Jesus has the power to bring all things under His control* (Philippians 3:21). All power has been given to Him. He can help us to control every evil thought, every physical impulse, to live graciously with others, to learn what we need to know to strengthen our faith, and to live closer to Him.

(8) Remember to *present our bodies as living sacrifices* (Romans 12:1). Every area of our lives—our careers, our service, our fitness plan, hobbies, recreation, family—each is to be placed under His control, directed into a unified oneness by the Holy Spirit.

(9) *Love the Lord.*

> *And behold, a certain lawyer stood up and put Him to the test, saying, "Teacher, what shall I do to inherit eternal life?"*
>
> *And He said to him, "What is written in the Law? How does it read to you?"*
>
> *And he answered and said, "You shall love the Lord your God with all your heart, and with all your soul, and with all your strength, and with all your mind; and your neighbor as yourself."*
>
> *—Luke 10:25-27*

> HEART *(kardia)*—the seat and center of all physical and spiritual life; the soul or mind, and so it is the seat of the thoughts, passions, appetites, desires, affections, purposes, endeavors; in other words, the INNER MAN.
>
> SOUL *(psyche)*—breath, the vital force which animates a body; that in which there is life, the seat of the feelings, desires, affections, and aversions.
>
> STRENGTH *(ischuros)*—might, power, faculty, ABILITY.
>
> MIND *(dianoia)*—intellect, understanding, imagination, insight, comprehension.
>
> We are to *love the Lord our God* with every fiber of our entire beings, and with every resource at our disposal.

This is that for which we strive. It is that for which Paul strove. Putting Christ in the center, and loving God with all of our being, is to be our New Purpose.

Study Questions

(1) What is it, in your opinion, that Paul has "not already obtained," of which he writes in Philippians 3:12?

(2) From Philippians 3:12, what does Paul state as a positive motivating force?

(3) What personal criticism is Paul answering in Philippians 3:12 and the first part of Philippians 3:13?

(4) From Philippians 3:12-16, list some characteristics of a mature Christian.

(5) In your own words, explain what "the goal for the prize of the upward call of God in Christ Jesus" is.

(6) (For you only, unless you want to share): What do I need to "forget" (to completely discard) about the past so that I can live a richer, more productive life in the present?

XI

Be Anxious For Nothing

Paul Challenges Us with a Great Twentieth Century Dilemma— Not to be Worried About Anything!

Text. . . . . Philippians 4:4-7.

Memory Verse. . . . . Philippians 4:6-7.

> *Rejoice in the Lord always; again I will say, rejoice! Let your forbearing spirit be known to all men. The Lord is near. Be anxious for nothing, but in everything by prayer and supplication with thanksgiving let your requests be made known to God. And the peace of God, which surpasses all comprehension, shall guard your hearts and your minds in Christ Jesus.*
>
> *—Philippians 4:4-7*

REJOICE!

Paul begins this marvelous passage with the command to rejoice. Indeed, throughout our entire study, he has laid the groundwork for the Philippians' rejoicing. In the last lesson, we will be looking closely at this almost exclusively Christian phenomenon. He has talked about how God molds us—that it is not entirely a work of our own. He has discussed the Christian's fearless attitude toward death. He has given them expansive insights into the causes of their disunity, and has guided them through thoroughly helpful advice for correcting that threat. He has introduced them to, and motivated them toward, a completely new value system in Christ, and has tutored them to a position of awareness and sophistication in respect to their enemies. He closes Chapter 3 by telling them that Jesus will change their bodies to be like His "by the exertion of the power that He has even to subject all things to Himself."

BE SWEETLY REASONABLE

So, of course, they and we are to rejoice! We have all the resources to live with power and triumph at our fingertips. Because of this, we are to demonstrate a "forbearing spirit" to all men. Barclay says of this word—ἐπιεικές *(epieikes)*—that it is one of the most untranslatable of all Greek words. It has been variously rendered "patience, softness, the patient mind, modesty, forbearance, gentleness, magnanimity, sweet reasonableness, equity, mildness, and lenience."

> *A man has the quality of "epieikes" if he knows when not to apply the strict letter of the law, when to relax justice, and introduce mercy...The Christian, as Paul sees it, is the man who knows that there is something beyond justice...Why should a man be like this? Why should he have this joy and gracious gentleness in his life? Because, says Paul, the Lord is at hand. If we remember the coming triumph of Christ, we can never lose our hope and joy...*
>
> *—Barclay, p. 75f*

Moreover, we are to let this beautiful influence be shown to *all* men.

There was a certain music competition held in Texas for high school-level students. The award money was substantial. Also at stake were scholarships and orchestral performances. Tensions and nerves were stretched as tightly as the violin strings on which the music was so beautifully being played.

One judge was overheard to say to the other, "Now, let's remember that these are very young students. If they suffer a memory slip, let's give them a chance to compose themselves, glance at the music, and have another go at it."

This happened with several contestants. The judges graciously demonstrated understanding and patience. Later, when the winners were announced, there was little bitterness or disappointment because the judges had previously been filled with magnanimity, when the "letter of the law" would normally have dictated instant disqualification. They had displayed "epieikes."

DO NOT WORRY

Because the Lord is close and His power is available, Paul then makes one of the most astonishing commandments in the New Testament:

Be anxious for nothing.

In Matthew 6:25-34, Jesus Himself discusses the material concerns which have always dominated the cares of most men. He almost pleads with us to believe in the care, the concern, the love, and the protection of the Father.

> *For all these things the Gentiles eagerly seek; for your heavenly Father knows that you need all these things.*
>
> —*Matthew 6:32*

He understands that these are a real and legitimate source of anxiety. But, like Jesus, Paul says, "Have no anxiety about anything."

But we will, of course. That is the human way. If we *never* had concern for any affairs, we would never take any precautions to protect ourselves and our families against poverty, illness, accident, or natural disaster. Of course, we will be anxious.

This Greek word, μεριμνᾶτε *(merimnate)* comes from a word meaning "to divide the mind." So Paul really is saying not to be distracted, not to let your mind be torn apart in all directions. It is also defined as "solicitude, or even grief; to care; cares, as the worrying and tormented cares which belong to human life."

The New Testament realizes that human life is swayed by care. The exhortation not to worry presupposes that every man naturally cares for himself and his life. This is by no means ruled out as illegitimate. Indeed, it is accepted that man is concerned about himself and that he strives after things. But the "why" and "wherefore" of his concern are given a new orientation; and so, too, is his understanding of himself and his life.

HOW?

To avoid this "torn apart mind," Paul gives us the key:

> *...but in everything by prayer and supplication with thanksgiving let your requests be made known unto God.*
>
> *—Philippians 4:6b*

Do not be anxious about anything, he says; and that means *anything!* (Easy to say; hard to do!) We call it "stress"—it eats away at our stomachs, gives us migraine headaches, and may cause some forms of cancer. It certainly contributes to high blood pressure, which is directly related to heart disease and stroke.

Say it again, Paul?

Don't be anxious—torn apart, distracted, under stress—about anything; but you will be, sometimes. So, in everything—and that means all these "anythings" we mentioned before—with prayer and supplication, let your requests be made known to God.

In this short sentence, Paul is teaching us a prodigious amount about prayer. It almost seems as if he is being repetitive in most of our English translations. However, he uses three distinct Greek words that bear closer comparison.

> *...but in everything, by prayer* (προσευχή: proseuke) *and supplication* (δέησις: de-ay-sis), *with thanksgiving, let your requests* (αἴτημα: ai-tay-ma) *be made known to God.*

> *Proseuke*—denotes prayer comprehensively, a general calling upon God; the mental posture of prayer; "face-to-face soul praying."
>
> *Deaysis*—frequently used for intercessory prayer or requests; an expression of piety in general; want, en-

> treaty, supplication; more often than "proseuke," a specific request; a specific sense of petitionary prayer. The Greek word for "please" comes from the same root word as this.
>
> *Aitayma*—requests, petitions, desires; used of individual petitions which constitute a prayer. In contrast to "deaysis," "aitayma" points to the specific content of the request.

So Paul says,

> *In everything, with a complete foundation or background of thanksgiving, take all kinds of prayer to God. Call upon His name in a reverent posture of prayer. Plead with, yearn for, and entreat His holy name. Pray for specifics: specific people and specific petitions. Whatever is bothering you, whatever is stressful or distracting—take it to the Lord in prayer, on any level.*

Some people think that it is wrong to pray for material concerns; that Christ told us to have the kind of faith that would lift us above this. If we are able, that is noble. But the idea really comes across in Philippians 4:6 that *whatever* is tearing one's mind apart is what he should be praying about. *In everything*—nothing too small that His fatherly concern cannot reach it, and nothing too great that His power cannot handle it. Fear, worry, and nervousness are all lost in the awareness that One is present who loves us more than we ever could possibly love ourselves, and whose resources are those of infinite wisdom and power. In the petitionary prayer which is based on anxiety, the man who prays attains a certain aloofness from his wishes when he puts them before God "with thanksgiving," and he thus finds liberation from care.

AND THE RESULTS...

> *And the peace of God, which surpasses all comprehension, shall guard your hearts and your minds in Christ Jesus.*
>
> —*Philippians 4:7*

The Peace of God! Volumes have been written, and still it is that which passes understanding. It is not given because we deserve it, nor is it always given in auspicious circumstances. Many people pray for the peace that passes understanding, not really realizing that what they want is a peace which is, in fact, readily understandable. They desire the peace which comes from an absence of conflict and trial—the security of a good income, an obedient family, absence from illness, good friends—i.e., a walk by quiet waters. These people want to dictate their own conditions of peace.

But what of Paul's circumstances? Riot, attack, physical abuse, persecutions of all kinds, imprisonment, the threat of a Roman ax—yet he had found God's peace. Can we understand this? Is it possible to comprehend this gift from the Lord—an island of peace in a chaotic sea? This gift truly surpasses all intellectual reasonableness.

The ground of peace rests in the fact that the Lord is near; that in His infinite power, He loves us with infinite love; and thus we are to approach Him in prayer surrounded by thanksgiving. God's peace, accessible to those in Christ, is an inward peace of the soul which is grounded in God's presence and promise. It quiets our hearts and our thoughts. Expanding the Greek of Paul's statement, it could read, "And the peace of God which passes all comprehension will throw up a garrison to guard your hearts and your minds in Christ Jesus." Both heart and mind are soothed to calm and rest, as Jesus stilled the sea in spite of wind and storm.

> *The peace of God is not of a negative quality. It is not soft with compromise and appeasement. Toward the threat of Satan, it is as hard as nails; it is made up of the spikes of the cross and blood, and a seal broken in defiance of Imperial Rome. It is the peace of superior might, the calm of absolute adequacy.*
>
> *—Herring, p. 99*

To acquire God's peace through prayer, remember three things:

(1) *The Presence of God.* He wants us to come to Him, to tell Him our troubles, and to draw closer to Him. He wants what is best and right for us.

(2) *The Promises of God.* He alone knows what is best for us. He knows the future and those affecting it. He has promised that nothing will ever separate us from Him.

(3) *The Power of God.* This alone can bring to pass what is best for us. It is unlimited and irresistible.

The man who remembers God's Presence, His Promises, and His Power will find His Peace.

Study Questions

(1) What would be the result of letting "all men know your forbearance?"

(2) In your own words, tell what the phrase "The Lord is at hand" means to you (Philippians 4:5).

(3) How is it possible to "have no anxiety" (Philippians 4:6)?

(4) What characteristic is to accompany all our prayers (Philippians 4:6)?

(5) Doesn't God already know our hearts and our needs? If so, then why pray?

(6) What is the purpose of prayer?

(7) Some have said that we should not pray for physical things. Why or why not?

(8) What does "the peace of God" mean to you (Philippians 4:7)? Why does it pass understanding?

(9) Should we dictate to God the terms of our "peace"? Why or why not? What kind of peace did Paul have? Can we have that same kind?

XII

Think on These Things

Our Intellectual Activities Are to Be on the Most Lofty Plane Possible, Which Will Ensure the Presence of the God of Peace

Text . . . . *Philippians 4:8,9.*

Memory Verse . . . . . *Philippians 4:8.*

INTRODUCTION

Some time ago, twice within one week, this author somewhat absent-mindedly picked up a newspaper and read a rather explicit article dealing with one aspect of seamy sex. One of the articles narrated a story of a young girl who had been tricked into coming to New York, and then had been forced, unwillingly, into prostitution. The other was about a young man who, after graduating from high school, had decided the straight life was not for him, and he had voluntarily gone into prostitution.

I do not pride myself for having read these articles. They sneaked into my consciousness through some mental back door which I had left unlocked. When I had finished reading each of them, the titles of which had appeared innocuous, I had felt polluted. They were graphically written and, although they were not classified as pornography by the world's standards, they affected my view of the world and of myself.

Yes—we must be cognizant of evil, of what is happening around us, of what it does to us and to our society, so that we can intelligently combat it. But for each of us there remains the fine line—how much "awareness" can we handle?

No matter how much one loves the Lord, how strong he is, how much he prays or serves his fellow man, his mind is touched by what he takes in. Television, radio, sound recordings, magazines, newspapers, novels, companionship—whatever we expose our minds to is what will affect us.

In our last lesson, we talked about not letting our minds be torn apart. But when they are, in everything with thanksgiving and with all kinds of prayers, we are to take it to the Lord. He will throw up a guard to protect our hearts and our minds. Our text for this lesson is an extension of this:

> *Finally, brethren, whatever is true, whatever is honorable, whatever is right, whatever is pure, whatever is lovely, whatever is of good repute, if there is any excellence and if anything worthy of praise, let your mind dwell on these things. The things you have learned and received and heard and seen in me, practice these things; and the God of peace shall be with you.*
>
> *—Philippians 4:8,9*

THE SETTING

Let us review the origins of Philippi. It was established during the reign of Philip, father of Alexander the Great, and was located in Macedonia, where both Philip and Alexander were born. It was steeped in Greek culture. This letter, then, was written to Greeks in the first Christian community to be established on the continent of Europe. The background of this verse is reminiscent of the way John appealed to the Greek understanding of the Logos in the opening of his Gospel.

In this culture, as the children were learning their lessons, they would copy lists of words, much as our children do today. But their lists were lists of virtues and vices. This list of words which Paul gives these Greeks here is similar to the list of the ancient Greek virtues; they are not uniquely Christian, but overall Paul is telling them that "this, in your background, is good; use it to bring peace."

THE ISSUES OF LIFE

> *Keep thy heart with all diligence; for out of it are the issues of life.*
>
> —*Proverbs 4:23 (KJV)*

All actions, motives, emotions, and relationships begin in the mind. The following list is by no means comprehensive, but is intended to stimulate thoughts along this line.

(1) Civilization
  (a) Laws
  (b) Hospitals
  (c) Museums
  (d) Libraries
  (e) Schools

(2) Creativity
  (a) Scientific Inventions and Discoveries
  (b) Fine Arts
  (c) Performing Arts
  (d) Literature
  (e) Ideas

(3) Personality
  (a) Emotions
  (b) Goals
  (c) Good Works
  (d) Praise
  (e) Love
  (f) Lies
  (g) Deceit

(4) False Religion

(5) Anti-Social Behaviors
  (a) Crimes
  (b) Wars
  (c) Antagonism
  (d) Anger
  (e) Psychosomatic Illness

These *are* the issues of life. This list could be expanded and subdivided many times over, of course, but every item originates within the mind of some individual. Small wonder that we are commanded to monitor what goes into our minds.

> *It is a law of life: when a man thinks of something often enough, he will come to the stage when he cannot stop thinking about it.*
>
> *—Barclay, p. 79*

WORDS TO BUILD

(1) *As to what's left*—Τὸ λοιπόν *(toh loipon:* the things remaining)—As to what remains to be said about this matter of peace, here is what I want you to do—dwell on the following things.

(2) *Whatever is true*—ἀληθής (*alaythas*)—In John 14:6, Jesus speaks of Himself as being truth. He is the ultimate in unchangeableness, as opposed to the world.

> *The things of this world are deceptive and illusory, often promising what they can never perform.*
>
> *Barclay, p. 79*

Sift out and learn about what is true; then let your mind dwell on those things.

(3) *Whatever is honorable*—σεμνά (*semna*)—a very difficult word to translate. In addition to being rendered "honorable," we have "august," "venerable," "worthy," "noble," "reputable," "worthy of reverence," and "nobly serious." It is associated with the dignity of holiness.

> *When used to describe a man, it describes a person who moves throughout the world as if it were the Temple of God...There are things which are flip-*

> *pant, cheap, and attractive to the light-minded; but it is on things which are serious and dignified on which the Christian will set his mind.*
>
> *—Barclay, p. 79*

(4) *Whatever is right*—δίκαιος (*dikaios*)—just, equitable, fair, responsible.

A man who can be described with "dikaios" is the one who gives to God and men their due; a man who squarely faces his duty, and then performs it. It goes back to a right relationship with God.

(5) *Whatever is pure*—ἅγιος (*hagios*)—pure, chaste, modest, innocent, blameless. When this word appears as a noun in the New Testament, it is usually translated "saint." It represents here that which is so pure and clean that it can be brought into God's presence and used in His service.

(6) *Whatever is lovely*—προσφιλῆ (*prosphilay*)—The only time this word is used in the New Testament. Synonyms—friendly, amicable, grateful, acceptable, attractive, pleasing, that which calls forth love.

> Winsome *is the best translation of all...The mind of the Christian is set on the lovely things—kindness, sympathy, forbearance—so he is a winsome person, whom to see is to love.*
>
> *—Barclay, p. 80*

The Greek roots literally translate "pros" as "near toward, face to face," and "philay" to be "friendship love." So, "prosphilay" is "face-to-face like"!

(7) *Whatever is of good report*—εὔφημα (*euphema*)—of good omen; auspicious, gracious, commendable, laudable, reputable. (Harrell: attractive or appealing, fair-sounding. Moffatt: high-toned; whatever has a good name.) One version has the reading, "Whatever things are well-spoken of."

We should dwell on, and pass along, the things which are fit for God to hear.

(8) *If there is any excellence*—The last two words under consideration seem to be all-encompassing ideas which apply to all of the former ones. Paul is saying, "If there is anything that covers excellence in all of the above..."

The Greek word ἀρετὴ (*arete*), from all of Paul's writings, only occurs once, and that here in Philippians 4:8. It means goodness, good quality of any kind, virtue, moral excellence, and uprightness. In classical Greek, it meant excellence of any kind. It was applied to the physical excellence of an animal or an athlete, excellence of fertile soil, and the courage of a soldier. He was using what was excellent in pagan terms to apply to their higher-mindedness in Christ.

(9) *If there is anything worthy of praise*—ἔπαινος (*epainos*)—ground or reason of praise or commendation. Every good man is lifted up by the praise of good men.

> *The Christian will live in such a way that he will neither conceitedly desire nor foolishly despise the praise of good men.*
>
> *Barclay, p. 81*

So Paul is saying that whatever is ground to be commended, and whatever is of a very high quality in everything around you...

THINK ON THESE THINGS

This is not something which merely goes in one ear and out the other. This verb means to think upon, ponder, analyze it carefully, and then make it a part of your life. Act on it! Discipline your mind to move in the realms of elevated thought.

> *We are destroying speculations and every lofty thing raised up against the knowledge of God, and we are taking every thought captive to the obedience of Christ.*
>
> *—2 Corinthians 10:5*

(1) *WHAT*—Then Paul says, "What you have learned and received and heard and seen in me, do." So many verbs, just heaped together! These too are part of the test for what goes into our minds. The Philippians did not have the scriptures as we do today. Righteousness in the early church depended on precept and example—Paul is drawing on every resource at his disposal and theirs to help bring them to a mature understanding of what was good and fitting. He has said, "You know these; you learned them, and received them into your lives because you heard them and saw them in me." In the vernacular of today, we would say, "Now, go for it!"

What are we to learn? What are we to make a part of ourselves? What are we to see and hear? The answer is also in Colossians 3:1,2:

> *If then you have been raised up with Christ, keep seeking the things above, where Christ is, seated at the right hand of God. Set your mind on the things above, not on the things that are on earth.*

Let us set our minds on those things which are true which will never let us down the rest of our lives, but continue to lift us up when we think on them.

Let us dwell on serious, lofty, and noble matters which hold within their dignified nature something which demands reverence and respect.

We want to take into our lives thoughts which will help us squarely to face and execute our duty to God and man, for we have obligations to both. We want to keep our lives in such a pure, uncluttered condition that they can be brought into God's presence and used in His service at any time.

We also want to think thoughts which will produce the kind of beauty in our lives that those with whom we come in contact can see Jesus. We can help them to feel accepted and comfortable in our presence. It is a part of the "sweet reasonableness" Paul talked about in verse 5. We want our speech to be gracious, high-toned, fit for God and man to hear, gentle and long-suffering.

(2) *WHY*—These high-toned thoughts energize us and make us feel alive. Those who have not tried this way of thinking might be trapped into saying, "Well, that might be fine for special moments and special times, but I've got to live in the real world, dealing with real problems, facing real situations, and I can't have my mind off in the wild blue somewhere all the time, thinking wonderful thoughts."

Au contraire, mon cher! Why not? Admittedly, this type of thinking takes discipline, and anything that takes discipline is not wrought overnight. But these thought patterns provide us with the strength and energy to cope with "Erma Bombeck" days, with everyday problems which drag us down, effectively depleting our inner resources.

Another more compelling reason is that, as a Christian, my mind belongs to God. To borrow from a song, I need to get my thoughts "up where the air is clear, up in the atmosphere" so that the Lord can mold, guide, and use them. He has set many and varied talents within the minds of mankind. Only comparatively few find and cultivate those talents. Only a very small percentage of these use their talents for the Lord. Humanity needs clear thinking and solid leadership grounded in Christ. Paul has drawn on every resource to show us how to become this type of Christian.

(3) *HOW*—

(a) Read your Bible; it is crammed with lofty thoughts, to say nothing of the invigorating Spirit which increasingly will work His way into and in your life.

(b) Pray that the Lord will help you discipline your mind in this direction. If an individual is in the habit of stuffing every morsel of food he sees into his mouth, his body quickly will show the results for the world to see. If one is in the habit of stuffing everything that comes along into his mind, the world can shortly see this in his life as well—his speech, his demeanor, his values, even his dress. God will help us along with anything we have chosen which is His will—higher-mindedness certainly is.

(c) Learn where the "off" button is on the television set, and then practice every day to see how fast you can apply your fingers to it. In just one short week, your timing should improve dramatically.

(d) Be discriminating in the music you listen to. Music has a way of grabbing us and saturating our souls long after the presentation is over. Even music without words carries messages and emotions. This author is, alas, a complete victim of the music heard. So this must be monitored carefully. Some lives may not be so affected, but the music we listen to must be considered.

(e) It *should* be comparatively easy to monitor what we read. When it comes time to renew that magazine subscription, if the magazine represents something less than your best aspirations, simply forget where your stamps are. The price of stamps is scandalous; are you sure that magazine is worth it? What about cheap paperbacks? There are excellent paperbacks on practically every subject—home and family living, do-it-yourself projects, self-improvement, interpersonal relationships, etc.—and even good literature in the fiction category. Why waste your time, money, and growth potential on one which is going to do nothing except rob you of these and provide a temporary cheap thrill? Set a goal to read for uplifting permanence.

(f) Most of us, at some point in our molding, have been reared to look at the Bible through world-colored glasses. This author was told by a "faithful" Christian shortly after baptism, "Now, it's a good idea not to become too involved with religion. Psychologists tell us that religious people are often mentally ill"! People question Paul because of what they perceive his stand to be on "women's rights." They consider biblical principles on morality to be "bunk" because of the biblical stand against the tenets of the "sexual revolution." Fellow Christians, IT IS TIME TO START LOOKING AT THE WORLD THROUGH

BIBLE-COLORED GLASSES. Know what the Book says, and then judge what the world is feeding you—not vice versa. Your mind and what goes into it is the rudder which will steer the destiny of your Eternity Ship; GUARD IT!

AND THE GOD OF PEACE WILL BE WITH YOU.

This is Paul's favorite title for God (Romans 16:20; 2 Timothy 3:16, 1 Thessalonians 5:23). He also calls Him the God of hope, the God of patience, comfort, and consolation, and the God of love and peace (2 Corinthians 13:11). In our last lesson, the Peace of God was given to soothe the fragmented mind. But if we can raise our sights and elevate our thoughts, building in the process a core of strength and beauty, we will begin to have the kind of "inner man" which will prevent that "torn-apart" mind. We not only will be blessed with the Peace of God; we can be the dwelling of the God of Peace Himself. In all of Paul's titles for God, we find a God of consolation who not only puts an arm of understanding around our shoulders, but gives us the strength to face the world. The God of patience does not give us the ability to simply sit down and bear our circumstances, but the ability to rise and conquer. The God of comfort not only wipes away the tears, but helps us to face the world with steady eyes. The God of love will never let us go. He helps the penitent to cease sinning without casting Him off.

Seek the lofty life by dwelling on lofty thoughts, and this Great God of Peace will be with you.

The pleasantest things in the world are pleasant thoughts; and the great art in life is to have as many of them as possible.

—Bovel

Study Questions

(1) What are your favorite scriptures to "think on" when things are "down?"

(2) Name at least four benefits you can think of which come from thinking on higher things.

(3) We found solutions in Philippians 4:5-7 for meeting days of tension, trouble, frustration, failure, and increased pressure. What rules are given in Philippians 4:8,9 for making these solutions effective?

(4) Find two scriptures in the Bible describing something:

   (a) True.
   (b) Just.
   (c) Pure.
   (d) Lovely.
   (e) Gracious.
   (f) Excellent.
   (g) Praiseworthy.

Think on These Things

(1) Absorb that which is true into your life—it will never let you down.

(2) Think on the things which are honorable, lofty, dignified, and serious—they will lift you above the mundane.

(3) Think on the things which will motivate you toward fulfilling your duty to God and man—they will make you valuable.

(4) Think about the things which will keep you pure and unsullied in this life—they will help you to preserve the preciousness of your reputation.

(5) Take in the things which make you lovely—they will help others to see Christ in you.

(6) Listen to and pass on those things which are of good report, fit for God to hear—they will make your speech blessed to the hearer.

(7) Strive for excellence and beauty in every activity, every product of your hands or your mind, every relationship, and every meditation.

(8) Whatever is worthy of commendation, give it speedily and wholeheartedly. Rejoice with those who achieve both great and small things. Neither seek nor shun praise, genuinely given, from others.

For every one who asks receives, and he who seeks finds, and to him who knocks it shall be opened.

—Matthew 7:8

XIII

Content in Whatever State

Paul Presents Us with a 20th Century-Sized Challenge— To Be Content Within the Circumstances In Which We Find Ourselves

Text .... *Philippians 4:10-13.*

Memory Verse ..... *Philippians 4:13.*

Two lessons ago, we studied Paul's access to the peace that exceeds understanding. His way to peace carried us over the broad avenues of prayer, of pleading with God, and of being explicit in those prayers. In the last lesson, we learned that to be accompanied by the God of peace, we needed to make lofty thinking, high ideals, and noble actions a very real part of our lives.

In this lesson, we are going to take a closer look at the results of these actions.

OUR TEXT

> *But I rejoiced in the Lord greatly, that now at last you have revived your concern for me; indeed, you were concerned before, but you lacked opportunity. Not that I speak from want; for I have learned to be content in whatever circumstances I am. I know how to get along with humble means, and I also know how to live in prosperity; in any and every circumstance I have learned the secret of being filled and going hungry, both of having abundance and suffering need. I can do all things through Him who strengthens me.*
>
> —*Philippians 4:10-13*

Contentment!—that illusion which, when we seek it, forever seems to be just beyond our grasp! If one is young, he usually seeks it in the accumulation of wealth. If he is old, he often seeks it in the guise of health and physical security. If contentment is interrupted by tragedy and grief, the seeker's comments are usually punctuated by the phrases beginning with, "If only..."

Shakespeare had a comment about contentment:

> *My crown is in my heart; not on my head; Not decked with diamonds, and Indian stones For to be seen.*
>
> *My crown is called content; a crown it is That seldom kings enjoy.*
>
> —King Henry VI, *Part III*

Shakespeare, at least, knew where contentment dwells—in the heart.

PAUL'S CHARACTERISTICS OF CONTENTMENT

Paul teaches us many things about contentment in this scripture:

(1) *That abundance is a state of mind*—When asked, "Who is the wealthiest man?", Socrates replied, "He who is content with the least, for self-sufficiency is nature's wealth." The most secure person is the one who can get along with the least. We all know people, supposed owners of many possessions, whose possessions own them.

They have to—paint it, clean it, insure it, repair it, polish it, re-upholster it, fuel it, lock it up, buy batteries for it, hide it, burglar-proof it, replace it, rebuild it, mend it, water it, walk it, feed it, vacuum it, dust it, chlorinate it, file it, mop it, launder it, iron it, store it, moth-proof it, oil it, freeze it, fence it, bleach it, thaw it, can it, wash it, wind it, prune it, mow it, brush it, invest it, frame it, mail it, return it, lose weight so they can get into it, save it, tune it, align it, take it to the vet, record it, and throw it away!

But Paul said he had learned to live in contentment with plenty as well. It is nice to own things and to have them for your use and God's, but that is not where contentment lies.

(2) *That want is a state of mind*—There is an old saying—"Them that wants, gets, and wants some more."

Eleanor Roosevelt was said to have been the possessor of a knack for buying *the* perfect Christmas gift. When asked her guidelines for the purchase of such, she replied, "It is always preferred to give the person what he wants the most; but that is not always possible. The second best choice is to give him one more of what he already has the most of."

If a person is truly in desperate physical need, finding contentment is made more difficult. But if physical needs are met, there is no guarantee contentment will follow. Want is a relative term.

Jerry Hogg, a former missionary to Africa, mentioned in conversation recently that most of the natives in Africa have never even seen, much less owned, most of the things which we throw away—a tin can, a glass jar, an empty aerosol can, a cardboard box, etc. Our list of supposed needs far outstrips their most fantastic wishes.

> *But godliness actually is a means of great gain, when accompanied by contentment. For we have brought nothing into the world, so we cannot take anything out of it either. And if we have food and covering, with these we shall be content.*
>
> *—1 Timothy 6:6-8*

(3) That what happens to us in this life is largely unimportant—Political situations, civic dealings, the entertainment glut, health considerations, financial problems, family matters—all are aspects of our life styles which may involve us deeply. At times, each may enmesh us out of proportion to the others. But these things pale into insignificance beside the great truths that God is in control; that eternity with Christ is that for which we are to strive; and that here on this earth, each of us is to be the servant, possessing the Mind of Christ. It is not what happens *to* us which is important, but how we react to it. If something negative happens, a lesser man will treat it as a calamity; a greater man will consider it a challenge. Paul knew truly that the things which happen to us are really *not very important.*

For I consider that the sufferings of this present time are not worthy to be compared with the glory that is to be revealed to us.

—*Romans 8:18*

THE HUMAN CONDITION

An important point which 20th century Americans need to absorb is that this age of affluence into which we are placed and which we have helped to create is largely an artificial condition in the history of humanity. In the story of civilization from the dawn of recorded time, and in third world countries today, the norm has been poverty, disease, natural calamities, high infant mortality, civil warfare, famine, etc.; in other words, the Human Condition. A society at peace, widespread general health, plentiful food, a high standard of living and education, the expectation that each child will live to adulthood—until the 20th century, this type of life style was unheard of, much less taken for granted. *We are living in an age of the exception, rather than the norm.* Most 20th century westerners have neither concept of nor appreciation for historical reality. Historically, we live in a Shangri-La of material blessings.

To approximate Paul's contentment, then, we have a double challenge: face the circumstances he had to face (see 2 Corinthians 6:4-10 and 11:23-33), then subtract modern medical, mechanical, and electronics technology, the information and communications explosion, and the advances in every field imaginable, and one has some idea of the challenge of *his* contentment. Perhaps in an age such as ours, we have spawned so many "advances" that these, in turn, have nurtured their own share of over-expectations.

OVER-EXPECTATIONS

Discontent remains a work of Satan; in our society, his tools are those of the media which promise, both in advertising and regular programming, that many products and activities will hand over more than they actually ever can or will.

We expect more miles for less gas, so we are discontent.

We expect more money for less work, so we are discontent.

We expect more recognition for less effort, so we are discontent.

We expect more progress in less time, so we are discontent.

We expect more response for less communication, so we are discontent.

We expect better behavior for less praise, so we are discontent.

We expect more obedience for less attention, so we are discontent.

We expect more romance for less commitment, so we are discontent.

We expect more pleasure for less consequence, so we are discontent.

Paul seems to be saying, "Take what comes, whether material or circumstantial. Know that it is all His, and that He is in control. Never expect more than actually comes from a situation or thing."

THE SOLUTION

To man's way of thinking, no person in his reasonable mind would be able to be content in *whatever* circumstances he finds himself. Most of us dream of some condition which precludes our contentment. Fill in the blank for yourself:

I would be content if ____________________.

The trap we fall into is that if and when this condition is met, something else will crowd into that blank, and we are discontent once more. But Paul has found the source of contentment.

> *Therefore I am well content with weaknesses, with insults, with distresses, with persecutions, with difficulties, for Christ's sake; for when I am weak, then I am strong.*
>
> *—2 Corinthians 12:10*

In his weakness, he has learned to stand on the Lord's strength, which fills him with the knowledge that predicates contentment. He goes on in Philippians to say that it is a mystery, but because of his many experiences in Christ, he has been empowered. In this present text, Paul literally says that he has been initiated into the mystery of contentment. The word which he uses in verse 12, translated "I have learned the secret," is the word which was used to describe initiation into the mystery religions. This is the only place in the New Testament where it is used. So he says, "I have been initiated through my experiences in Christ into the mystery of knowing how to face any situation."

His contentment was not a passive settling back, meekly enduring whatever life dealt him. It came from a very real security in being able to face squarely any situation with confidence, poise, and grace.

In Philippians 4:13, we come face to face with Paul's source of power:

> *I can do all things through Him who strengthens me.*

Paul's word for "do" is the same word from which we get our word "dynamite." He says, "My dynamic comes from His strength. He is my prime mover, my motivation." Furthermore, Paul includes all things. Can we say that of ourselves?

Christ said that all power had been given to Him in Heaven and on earth. Paul said that we would not be tempted (or tried) above that which we are able to bear (1 Corinthians 10:13). But the following verse is the one which gives me the most courage:

> *Now to Him who by the power at work within us is able to do far more abundantly than all that we ask or think, to Him be the glory in the church...*
>
> *—Ephesians 3:20,21a (RSV)*

There is a power, a dynamic, at work within us, if we let it abide and work there.

BECAUSE GOD'S POWER IS IN US:

We can learn to be self-sufficient in any circumstance.

We can live dynamic and powerful lives.

We can meet temptation.

We can rejoice in tribulation.

We can face death, adverse circumstances, ill health, rebellious children, the day-to-day vicissitudes of daily living...because God's power is in us.

Again, this comes through a right relationship with God.

...And may be found in Him, not having a righteousness of my own derived from the Law, but that which is through faith in Christ, the righteousness which comes from God on the basis of faith...

—Philippians 3:9

And from whence comes faith?

So faith comes from what is heard, and what is heard comes by the preaching of Christ.

—Romans 10:17 (RSV)

TO GROW TOWARD CONTENTMENT

I was a lukewarm Christian until I began to study. When a Christian reads, he can either read *about* God, or he can read to become *like* God. He can study in order to teach or dispute the scriptures, or he can study to make God's living word a real part of his soul, to let it mold him. God's dynamic is not in dead words. Why is the Bible called "the Living Word"?

(1) Its truths are timeless and changeless, and they continue to apply to every facet of our lives.

(2) It itself is everlasting.

(3) It changes lives when studied.

(4) It gives us the power to live positively and optimistically.

If one accepts Paul's challenge to learn to be content, God is not just going to drop this on him. As he feeds on His word day by day and grows stronger little by little, this challenge will gradually be met.

> *Therefore we do not lose heart, but though our outer man is decaying, yet our inner man is being renewed day by day.*
>
> —*2 Corinthians 4:16*

By renewing the inner man with prayer, study, and your daily walk with God, His power in you will grow, and you will begin to discover His contentment, regardless of outward circumstances.

Study Questions

(1) What is the most difficult circumstance in your life over which you are discontent?

(2) Ponder 1 Timothy 6:6-8. Considering what he says in verses 7 and 8, what does he mean by verse 6? What kind of gain?

(3) Could we be abased (brought low, humbled) as Paul said in verse 12 and be content? How?

(4) Study 2 Corinthians 9:8. Does this give us a clue as to why we live in abundance at times?

(5) Consider Hebrews 12:5-11. Does this give us a clue as to why we experience difficult times?

(6) In 2 Corinthians 12:7-10, what does Paul say is the source of his strength?

(7) What are some of the "all things" for which the Lord has extended His strength to you? Do you commit "all things" to Him in calm times as well as tempestuous ones?

XIV

Rejoice!

The Undeniable Christian Philosophy of Life—Our Joy in Christ

Text..............*Philippians 4:4.*

Supplementary.....*Philippians 1:18,19, 2:17,18, 3:1, 4:10.*

Memory Verse.....*Philippians 4:4.*

The Greeks, who held the keys of enlightenment and learning, sought many ways to improve mankind:

(1) For his physique, the Olympic and other games were the most refined and strenuous events to crown the athletic world.

(2) For man's social nature, the Greeks evolved complex ethical and moral systems.

(3) For his mind, they developed finely tuned systems of the arts, sciences, all forms of literature, history, and smatterings of almost every other academic pursuit.

(4) For man's religious nature, there was the Pantheon—that collection of gods of which one would surely suit the tastes and needs of each individual in any situation.

However, with every system they developed, that system, when carried to its logical consequences, wreaked havoc with man's soul.

The Greeks were in darkness.

The Romans, who held the keys of political control, sought to better the lot of mankind through a semblance of peace through better government. To maintain this government, they had built excellent roads throughout the Empire. Through superbly disciplined troops and an efficient legal system, they were able to enforce a brand of international peace for an unprecedented time and expanse of territory.

However, the lives of the Romans generally were extremely corrupt (see Romans 1:18-32; 2 Peter 2:10-14). The worth of human life for all but free men (i.e., women, children, and slaves) was the price of what that soul would bring in the marketplace. Husbands possessed life-or-death power over their wives and children. A child could be murdered, no questions asked, at the whim of a parent. A wife could be cast into the street with no support or any legal rights at the slightest supposed annoyance of her husband. A slave could be disposed of at the least indication of illness, clumsiness, or incompetence.

The Romans were in darkness.

The Jews, custodians of the Law and the Prophets, were in a covenant relationship with God. Having been granted return from exile, they were under the government of Rome, but retained their rights both to worship and to conduct their daily affairs as they pleased. However, they overlooked the weightier matters of their Law: justice, mercy, and faith (Matthew 23:23). They neglected the care of widows and orphans. They counted their own righteousness in terms of their observances of ordinances, focusing on the externals of their Law, their interpretations of scripture, and their man-made traditions, rather than allowing their zeal for those scriptures to lead them to God's heart. They looked forward to an earthly Messiah to restore to them the material and political power attained by David and Solomon.

The Jews were in darkness.

Darkness was upon the face of the whole earth. And the Spirit of God was moving over the face of the whole earth.

And God said, "Let there be light," and there was light. And God saw that the light was good; and God separated the light from the darkness...

The people who walk in darkness will see a great light; those who live in a dark land, the light will shine on them.

And the light shines in the darkness; and the darkness did not comprehend it...There was the true light which, coming into the world, enlightens every man. He was in the world, and the world was made through Him, and the world did not know Him...

And (He) became flesh, and dwelt among us, and we beheld His glory, glory as of the only begotten from the Father, full of grace and truth...

No man has seen God at any time; the only begotten God, who is in the bosom of the Father, He has explained Him...

The darkness is passing away, and the true light is already shining.

—*Genesis 1:3,4; Isaiah 9:2; John 1:5,9,10,14,18; 1 John 2:8b*

The force of the life of Jesus Christ and the power of His Resurrection burst upon the pagan world of darkness with a dynamism which is difficult, if not impossible, for us to contemplate. In the places the Gospel has been taught, each one living today has grown up with the principles of the Gospel at least available to him.

But when Nicodemus came to Jesus by night, he had seen a Light not seen before. As Jesus spoke of the spiritual rebirth, Nicodemus' heart must have leapt within him. Hoping that the Holy Spirit will forgive the misquotation:

For just as the lightning comes from the east, and flashes even to the west, so was the coming of the Son of Man.

—*borrowed from Matthew 24:27*

A new beginning—one which had forever eluded the hopes of mankind! Cleansing from sin for a new start! The creation of a new, unheard-of kind of love! The freedom from the guilt-ridden observance of the Old Law, to the keeping of a new and perfect Law of Liberty, where God Himself cleanses the heart with a divine act of grace, and humankind is not burdened with the impossible task of making itself righteous!

A new start—one which liberated the meaning of *life* itself from the everyday existence of eating, sleeping, procreating and dying, and which gave life a spirit, an eternal dimension, and the power to soar above the shackles of death!

The Light—that which shows evil to be what it is, and provides a straightforward illuminated example of what the Father Himself is like!

These timeless truths are relevant and absolutely essential for each generation. No wonder the repeated injunction to "Rejoice!" given throughout Philippians! No wonder the grief and tears visited upon Paul as his tender young converts often failed to glimpse the True Light!

PAUL'S REASONS FOR REJOICING (as stated in Philippians)

(1) Philippians 1:18,19.

> *What then? Only that in every way, whether in pretense or in truth, Christ is proclaimed; and in this I rejoice, yes, and I will rejoice. For I know that this shall turn out for my deliverance through your prayers and the provision of the Spirit of Jesus Christ...*

Paul rejoiced that Christ was being proclaimed. And these are grounds for our rejoicing as well.

(a) Salvation and all it meant was being brought into people's lives.

(b) A better life here became available to them as Christ began to lift them to greater heights.

(c) A better life to come is also the promise to the Christian (Philippians 1:21-23).

(d) Christ helped them to stand in the face of tribulation (Philippians 1:29-30).

(e) Their acceptance made available to them the spiritual beauty of unified believers...

...and in these things, Paul rejoiced.

(2) Philippians 2:17,18.

> *But even if I am being poured out as a drink offering upon the sacrifice and service of your faith, I rejoice and share my joy with you all. And you too, I urge you, rejoice in the same way and share your joy with me.*

Paul had an all-encompassing ministry—that of preaching the Word. He was rejoicing because the Philippians were sharing that ministry and working alongside him in it. Even if he were to be sacrificed in Rome, he was rejoicing with them because they were standing fast, with or without him; and he implored them to rejoice with him.

What great cause for rejoicing when a work is begun, engaged in by Christians who pull together to start the work; then work together to make it a success! When the results of the work begin to come back, they become even stronger and more unified!

The Philippians were worried because of Paul's bonds; but as a beautiful fruit of his labors, they were to rejoice because they were standing fast. Their fellowship was beautiful; their relationship with Paul was beautiful; and their example to the world was beautiful! For all of these things, they were to rejoice—as are we—for these apply to us as well.

(3) Philippians 2:28.

> *Therefore I have sent him all the more eagerly in order that when you see him again you may rejoice and I may be less concerned about you.*

Paul rejoiced that Epaphroditus was spared and would be seeing them again. They, and we today, can rejoice that God is a merciful God, hearing the prayers of His saints.

(4) Philippians 4:10.

> *But I rejoiced in the Lord greatly, that now at last you have revived your concern for me; indeed, you were concerned before, but you lacked opportunity.*

In this verse, he expresses his gratitude that they had again shown their concern for him—not primarily because of financial gain, but because he was assured again that they were with him, both emotionally and materially.

All of us need the support and encouragement of those who are like-minded. We need constant reassuring of the fact that we are approved of and loved by those who mean the most to us. Those in mission fields, particularly, need the sustenance of other Christians. With emotional support, we can conquer anything set before us.

Paul had Christ, and in Him he could stand. But when his brethren also were supportive, Paul rejoiced. Today, we need the lesson of learning to be more openly loving, giving, and encouraging to those with whom we labor in Christ.

PROBLEMS, PROBLEMS!

In all of his letters, Paul writes time and time again of problems he was facing. In addition to physical persecutions, he was confronted repeatedly with atheists, doubters, and weak Christians dealing with the problems of suffering—causes which kept them from rejoicing.

He might have said, "How can I rejoice when ________________?"

In Philippians 4:4, Paul wrote the most difficult of words—"always"! He tells them to rejoice, and that "in the Lord." He knows of the trials, problems, frustrations, and tragedies of this life, so he inserts "always" and then says, "And again I say, 'Rejoice!' "

This context is not the place to enter into an involved discussion of the foreknowledge of God versus the free will of man. As finite human beings, we can never fully understand the relationship of what God causes, what He allows, what He prevents, and man's free choices in all of these. But Christians firmly believe that if we entrust our lives to Him, what happens to us will work out for our best interests. We need to pray some version of the following prayer:

> *Lord, I don't want to do what's wrong; I want to be free from sin; I want to do Your will completely. Keep me from evil and wrong judgment.*

Christians are never told that the situation will be changed *because* of our rejoicing; but because the Lord is at hand:

(1) We can be lifted above the situation;

(2) We ourselves can be changed; and

(3) We can be endowed with the strength to face the trial.

There are three main reasons we can rejoice in tribulation.

(1) Our *well-being* is important to God.

He does not give us everything we want, just as we do not give our children everything they want; it would not be good for us. As parents, for example, we give our children immunization shots. We train them to go to school and do their chores. For ourselves, we try to discipline our bodies.

We can rejoice in tribulations because we know these can bring us the discipline we need to grow more like the Lord and, hence, closer to Him.

(2) Our *salvation* is important to God.

He knows the full impact of the terror of sin. Because of this, He gave us Jesus, the initiator of salvation, and the Holy Spirit, who oversees our continued growth. He has given us everything we need to guarantee our salvation. But He has also built in parameters to our actions; if we go beyond these, we suffer. He provides physical suffering for physical transgression, emotional suffering for emotional transgression, and social suffering for social infractions. Most of the fruits of sin are simply the natural consequences of engaging in that action.

We can rejoice in tribulation when it keeps us from sinning. It can keep us humble; it keeps us sensitive to our fellow man; and it keeps us relying on God.

(3) Our *deaths* are important to God (Psalm 116:15).

Death is not the "worst thing" that can happen to us. Because of death, life is made precious. Because we have just "so much" time, we tend to put a value on the time we do have. If we experience the passing of a loved one, we tend to become much more aware of the value to us of the loved ones we have left. Even the death of a loved one, painful as that is, is necessary. It makes us more cognizant of the grief of others, more reliant on God, more aware of the value of our time, and especially aware of the urgency to spread the Gospel—to *every* creature.

God's ways are not our ways.
Suffering is the norm, not the exception.
The Christian is not guaranteed a trouble-free life; just the strength to rise above his troubles.

THE ABUNDANT LIFE

Paul knew the joyous life, the mood of cheerfulness, the serenity and calmness of spirit possible only to the soul stayed on God... There is no other ground of perpetual optimism that is not blind indifference.

—Robertson, p. 231

This philosophy of life, our joy in Christ, is not dependent on the emotion of the moment, but it is a decision, a settled principle. It is a deep-rooted fringe benefit of a faith in, and a commitment to, Christ. It is a below-the-surface anchor withstanding the storm-tossed waves on the surface.

I am come that they might have life and might have it abundantly.

—John 10:10b

Rejoice in the abundant life! The new abundance in Christ, where...

...happiness deepens to joy...
...enthusiasm deepens to commitment...
...kindness deepens to compassion...
...fondness deepens to love...
...belief deepens to faith...
...expectation deepens to hope...

...and where contentment deepens to peace. These underscore the abundant life—that which is the eternal life, in Christ.

Rejoice in the Lord, always; again I will say: Rejoice!
—Philippians 4:4

Study Questions

(1) What is the greatest cause for rejoicing in your life?

(2) List as many blessings as you can think of, and rejoice over these.

(3) List as many "unblessings" as you can think of. Can you rejoice in these? Why, or why not?

(4) (a) Paul rejoiced for two reasons in Philippians 1:18,19. What are they?
(b) What is the reason for rejoicing in Philippians 2:17,18?
(c) What is the reason for rejoicing in Philippians 2:28?
(d) What is the reason for rejoicing in Philippians 4:10? (careful—see Philippians 4:18)
(e) What is the reason for rejoicing in Philippians 1:3,4?

(5) Name some side effects of being in Christ which give you cause for rejoicing.

(6) Discuss practical ways to maintain an inner joy in the face of hardship.

Bibliography

Barclay, William, *The Letters to the Philippians, Colossians, and Thessalonians* (Philadelphia: Westminster Press, 1975).

Coffman, James V., *Commentary on Galatians, Ephesians, Philippians, and Colossians* (Austin: Firm Foundation, 1977).

Harrell, Pat, *The Letter of Paul to the Philippians* (Austin: R. B. Sweet Co., Inc., 1971).

Herring, Ralph A., *Studies in Philippians* (Nashville: Broadman Press, 1952).

Robertson, A. T., *Paul's Joy in Christ* (Grand Rapids: Baker Book House, 1979).

Shepherd, J. W., "Commentary on the Epistle to the Philippians" from *A Commentary on the New Testament Epistles*, David Lipscomb, Editor, Vol. IV (Nashville: Gospel Advocate, 1939).

Reference Materials

Kittel, Gerhard, editor, *Theological Dictionary of the New Testament* (Grand Rapids: Wm. B. Eerdman's Publishing Co., 1964).

Moulton, Harold K., *The Analytical Greek Lexicon Revised* (Grand Rapids: Zondervan, 1978).

Strong, James, *Exhaustive Concordance of the Bible* (Nashville: Thomas Nelson Publishers).

Thayer, Joseph H., *Greek-English Lexicon of the New Testament* (Grand Rapids: Baker Book House, 1977).

Appendix

Enemies of Inner Peace (Things That Weaken and Ruin the Inner Man)

(1) *Materialism:* An inordinate desire for things; interest in and preoccupation with things. Biblically, it is equated with covetousness, idolatry, and greed. It is depicted in Ecclesiastes 5:10; Matthew 6:19-21; Matthew 19:16-22; Luke 12:13-21; 1 Timothy 6:6-10, 17-20.

Antidote: Matthew 6:33.

(2) *Infantilism:* A process of retardation in intellectual growth and social development.

Symptoms: temper tantrums, self-centeredness, selfishness, anger, envy, jealousy, fault-finding, gossip, and stubbornness.

Antidote: 1 Corinthians 13:11.

(3) *Narcissism:* An inordinately high opinion of one's own personality and opinions; preoccupation with self. Loneliness breeds narcissism and often vice versa, and they each breed insecurity.

Antidote: Philippians 2:3,4; Romans 12:3.

(4) *Dogmatism:* The state or tendency of being extremely censorious of others. The state is manifested by such statements as "All who do not believe what I believe are ignorant" and "My point of view is the only point of view, and don't you dare disagree!" Truth is dogmatic, but one's treatment of truth should not be one of dogmatism.

Antidote: Romans 12:3,16; 2 Timothy 2:24-26.

(5) *Legalism:* Involving oneself with the externals, "the letter of the law," but devoid of purpose, heart, and spirit of the requirement. Also, involvement with the doctrines, commandments, and traditions of men; disputing over them, requiring them as rules for living and/or salvation. This mentality leads first to an assumption

that one can "work his way to heaven," and then to depression that grows from an awareness of personal failing and imperfection.

Antidote: Micah 6:8; 1 John 1:7-10, 2:1,2.

(6) *Dualism:* Having a split personality that so disguises the person that the only consistent pattern is the pattern of inconsistency...the distance between the "ought" and "is" involved with inconsistency, to the point of being "double-minded"; described in James 1:8.

Antidote: Colossians 3:1-3; Matthew 6:22-24.

(7) *Perfectionism:* Closely akin to legalism and dogmatism; intolerance of any defect in self or others; places priorities on projects, methods, and performance rather than on people, their thoughts, feelings, emotions, and potential.

Antidote: 1 Peter 3:18; Philippians 3:13,14.

(8) *Defeatism:* Pessimism destructively loosed in one's personality—"Woe is me...I can't..."

Antidote: Philippians 4:11-13.

(9) *Escapism:* The dodging or evading of reality and/or responsibility.

Symptoms: procrastination, daydreaming, laziness, television addiction, drug abuse, lying, exaggeration, desertion, compulsive excess, workaholism, "passing the buck," condemning others, mental breakdown (really usually "ego breakdown"), and suicide (the ultimate act of loneliness).

Antidote: Acts 17:30,31; Romans 12:1,2; Matthew 5:1-16.

All of the above are simply irresponsible attitudes and their resultant actions which men adopt in their approach to life, its relationships and responsibilities. Responsible attitude and action is the antidote to these.

—contributed by Ron Bryant